Willing Patriots

MEN OF COLOR IN THE FIRST WORLD WAR

Robert J. Dalessandro & Gerald Torrence

with Michael G. Knapp

Schiffer Military History
Atglen, PA

Acknowledgements

Although this book had two principal authors, it was truly a team effort. Without the council and knowledge of both Mike Knapp and Tom Fife this volume would not have been possible. Both men gave freely of their time to better the work. As with every historical endeavor, the vast holdings of the Army Heritage and Education Center and particularly the Military History Institute at Carlisle, Pennsylvania allowed us to shed light on often forgotten aspects of this topic. Our thanks go out to the many helpful members of the Army Heritage and Education Center staff; at the Military History Institute: Dr. Con Crane, Dr. Richard "Dick" Sommers, Dr. Art Bergeron, Rich Baker, Louise Arnold-Friend, and Molly Bompaine; at the Army Heritage Museum: Roger Durham, Jay Graybeal, Jim McNally and Chris Semancik; at Collection Management Directorate: Greg Statler and Jane Smith-Stewart. Dr. Mitch Yokelson at the National Archives provided invaluable information on unit types and locations – thanks! Numerous collectors provided advice and made their personal collections available to us: Gus Radle, Don Troiani, Steven Wagner and Kenneth V. Reece were especially helpful in providing photographs and materials from their collections. Tom Fife's willingness to share his rare and unpublished photograph collection enhanced this book beyond description. We are especially appreciative of the typing support provided by Teresa Highlands; our grateful thanks go out to our wives Tracie Torrence and Rebecca Dalessandro. Rebecca provided her usual magnificent editorial support with Major Ginger Shaw and Brandi Buchman rounding out the Carlisle editorial team. We could not have completed the manuscript without each of you! Finally, thanks to Bob Biondi at Schiffer Books for making this all look so easy!

Dedication

To the countless Americans of all races and genders who willingly served a Country that often did not provide them the promise of Freedom provided to their fellow citizens. Their patience and belief in an often imperfect Government made and continues to make America great. This book stands in tribute to the generation of these men and women who fought to make the "world safe for Democracy" And to their grand and great grandchildren who still fight for our Freedom today.

Book design by Robert Biondi.

Printed in China.
ISBN: 978-0-7643-3233-3

We are always looking for people to write books on new and related subjects. If you have an idea for a book, please contact us at the address below.

Published by Schiffer Publishing Ltd. 4880 Lower Valley Road Atglen, PA 19310 Phone: (610) 593-1777 FAX: (610) 593-2002 E-mail: Info@schifferbooks.com. Visit our web site at: www.schifferbooks.com Please write for a free catalog. This book may be purchased from the publisher. Please include $5.00 postage. Try your bookstore first.	In Europe, Schiffer books are distributed by: Bushwood Books 6 Marksbury Ave. Kew Gardens, Surrey TW9 4JF England Phone: 44 (0)20 8392-8585 FAX: 44 (0)20 8392-9876 E-mail: info@bushwoodbooks.co.uk www.bushwoodbooks.co.uk

CONTENTS

INTRODUCTION

Black Americans have a long history of taking up arms in defense of freedom and democracy in America. Their service is marked with courageous devotion to a nation which has not always acknowledged them as citizens and equals, and in whose interests and prosperity they have had less at stake.[1] Yet their service marks them as willing patriots. It may be said that the first shot that initiated the first great movement for human liberty[2] – the Revolutionary War – occurred not at Lexington in 1775, but five years earlier on March 5, 1770 at what is known today as the Boston Massacre. The leader of the citizens of this event was a black man, Crispus Attucks. He was the first upon whom the British soldiers fired, and the first to fall for American Independence. Estimates report that approximately 3,000 black soldiers served in the American Army during the Revolutionary War. Connecticut raised a black battalion, and Rhode Island first freed their slaves then stood up a regiment. Massachusetts fielded one company of black Americans bearing the special designation of "The Bucks." This company won fame and notoriety and, at the conclusion of the war, were the recipients of much praise from John Hancock. There were great individual contributions from such notables as Salem Poor, Titus Coburn and Alexander Ames, all of whom fought valiantly at the Battle of Bunker Hill. Of special note was the service rendered by Deborah Gannet, a black woman who enlisted under the name of Robert Shurtliff, in Captain Webb's company of the 4th Massachusetts Regiment. A resolution passed by the 1791 Massachusetts General Court proclaimed, Deborah exhibited an extraordinary instance of female heroism by discharging the duties of a faithful, gallant soldier, and at the same time preserving the virtues and chastity of her sex unsuspected and unblemished.[3]

In America's second war with Great Britain, the War of 1812, fully ten percent of Commodore Perry's crew was black at the Battle of Lake Erie. Commodore Perry praised these men stating they were brave, of good conduct, and absolutely insensible to danger. Except for the Battle of New Orleans, the majority of martial glory occurred on the seas, however New York State passed a resolution that authorized the formation of two black regiments. Other states recruited blacks heavily. At the Battle of New Orleans, General Andrew Jackson called the citizens of Louisiana to the field. This call to duty included free blacks. On December 18, 1814 General Jackson's commendatory was read to these black solders: "… I expected much from you; for I was not ignorant that you possessed qualities most formidable to an invading enemy … I knew well how you loved your native country, and that you, as well as ourselves, had to defend what man holds most dear-his parents, wife, children and property. You have done more than I expected … I found among you a noble enthusiasm, which leads to the performance of great things."[4]

In the contest with Mexico, incidents of bravery by black soldiers, and slaves serving as soldiers are a matter of record. Colonel Clay, the son of Henry Clay was struck from his horse at the Battle of Buena Vista. His servant, who was fighting alongside of him in the thick of battle, stayed with him, and in the face of overwhelming odds succeeded in carrying the mangled body of Colonel Clay from the field. There is evidence that the life of General Zachery Taylor was spared by the gallant actions of a slave at the Battle of Monterey. General Taylor was the intended target of a Mexican soldier, when the slave sprang between them, slew the Mexican and was wounded in the process. General Taylor later emancipated the slave.

General Order Number 1, issued on January 2, 1863, from the War Department, was President Lincoln's Proclamation of Emancipation. The seventh paragraph stated, "such persons of suitable condition, will be received into the service of the United States, to garrison forts, positions, stations, and other places, and to man vessels of all sorts in said service."[5] The eventual result was almost 200,000 black Americans served in the ranks of the Federal military arms during the Civil War. Their performance is well known, is of uniform excellence, and in some cases, legendary. Some of the most inspiring exploits in the annals of Civil War history include the campaigns of Port Hudson, Louisiana; Fort Pillow, Kentucky; and Fort

Wagner, South Carolina, where the fabled 54th Regiment Massachusetts Volunteer Infantry (Colored), wrapped itself in glory and honor in a most heroic manner. Ultimately, fifteen states raised volunteer regiments with the designation as U.S. Colored Troops (U.S.C.T.). Nine black regiments were present at Appomattox, VA on April 9, 1865 for the surrender of General Robert E. Lee's Army of Northern Virginia, to General Ulysses S. Grant. Six black regiments participated in the surrender of General Joseph E. Johnston's Army to General William T. Sherman. The 62nd U.S.C.T. pitched in during the last battle of the Civil War at Palmetto Ranch on May 15, 1865. As in past wars, there were also several exceptional individual contributions. Charles E. Nash enlisted in the 83rd Regiment, United States Chasseurs d'Afrique and became the regimental sergeant-major. He lost a leg while storming Fort Blakely, was honorably discharged, and afterwards became a member of congress. Lewis Douglas, the son of abolitionist Frederick Douglas, served in the 54th Massachusetts rising to the rank of sergeant-major. Major Martin R. Delany of the 104th U.S.C.T. is often credited with the distinction of being the first black commissioned officer. Major Frank M. Welch of the 5th Battalion (Colored) Connecticut National Guard became the highest-ranking black commissioned officer in the Connecticut National Guard. He began his service with the 54th Massachusetts, and as a sergeant in the regiment was wounded during the now legendary assault on Fort Wagner. By the conclusion of the Civil War, sixteen black solders received the Medal of Honor.

Owing to the valor and fitness of black soldiers so completely demonstrated in the Civil War, the War Department moved to increase the size of the Regular Army, resourcing fifty percent of the increase from black men. In 1866, eight new infantry regiments were authorized, of which four were black; the 38th, 39th, 40th and 41st Infantry Regiments. Additionally, four new cavalry regiments were recruited, of which two were black; the 9th and 10th Cavalry Regiments. In 1869 a reduction in the Regular Army prompted a consolidation of the infantry regiments. The 38th and 41st were combined to form the 24th Infantry Regiment; the 39th and 40th were consolidated into the 25th Infantry Regiment. The strength and designation of the cavalry regiments remained unchanged. These regiments performed gallantly bearing some of the most arduous duty including many Indian campaigns, earning the gallant moniker as the Buffalo Soldiers. Generals Miles and Merritt, famed commanders of the Indian Wars were "unstinting in their commendation of the valor and skill of Negro fighters."[6] It was these four regiments that represented black Americans in the Regular Army for the ensuing forty-eight years leading up to World War I.

In 1898, with the commencement of the Spanish American War, the four black Regular Army regiments were filled to their maximum strength to meet wartime demands. Once filled, no more blacks were accepted into the active military. To meet the insistence of black Americans for military service, Congress authorized the formation of ten black volunteer regiments called "immune" regiments. The ranks of these formations were filled with men who had lived in territories where the yellow fever and other malignant or malarial visitations had occurred, and who had suffered from them or shown evidences that they had in all probability would be immune from the diseases.[7] As a result of the policy to assign only white officers to these regiments, only four immunes were ultimately raised; the 7th, 8th, 9th, and 10th. However, several states did raise additional black units, many of them commissioning black officers to lead them. They were Companies A and B of the Indiana Infantry, the 33rd Kansas Infantry, a battalion of the 9th Ohio Infantry, the 3rd Alabama, 6th Virginia Infantry, and the 8th Illinois Infantry. The 8th Illinois was completely officered by black men. J.R. Marshall was its' first commander leading it through the Spanish-American War, and for a time serving as military governor of San Luis. Others included the North Carolina 3rd Infantry commanded by Colonel Charles Young and officered by black men throughout, and Company L of the 6th Massachusetts Infantry – a black company in serving in a white regiment. Owing to the brief time span of the Cuban campaigns, the majority of the action for the black serviceman devolved upon the Regulars. Colonel Theodore Roosevelt proclaimed the performance of the 9th and 10th Cavalry Regiments reflected great honor on all Americans. The historical records of these Buffalo Soldiers at San Juan Hill are replete with accounts of gallant, brave, and exceptional fighting effectiveness. The verdict of some accounts attributes the 9th and 10th Cavalry Regiments with saving the Rough Riders from annihilation. Following the Cuban Campaign, black troops rendered distinguished service during the Philippine uprisings – at times holding garrisons there to preserve order.

For three years, President Woodrow Wilson avoided entering the Great War in Europe. However; by 1917, America could no longer sit on the sidelines, while freedom and democracy hung in the balance in Europe. This contest was a struggle for humanity – of Republicanism against Absolutism, for the rights of small nations, and to make the world safe for democracy.[8] The stakes were tremendous, and extended beyond the bounds of Europe, across the expanse of the Atlantic, and into the United States. Try as he might, the stresses imposed by the European conflict, and especially the actions of the Germans; particularly their blatant and unrepentant use of U-boats against American merchant ships and the infamous Zimmerman letter, drew America into this world-wide struggle. On April 6th 1917, President Wilson declared war against Imperial Germany. At this time, there were some 20,000 trained, equipped, drilled and experienced Negro Soldiers in uniform. About 10,000 were in the ranks of the four Regular Army Regiments, 9th and 10th Cavalry Regiments and the 24th and 25th Infantry Regiments. The remaining numbers were enrolled in National Guard units in several states. These National Guard units were: the 8th Illinois Regiment, the 15th New York Regiment, the 1st Separate Battalion of Washington, DC, the 1st Separate Company of Maryland, the 9th Ohio Battalion, the 1st Separate Company of Connecticut, Company L of the Massachusetts National Guard, and Company G of the Tennessee National Guard. At the outset, black Americans who volunteered for service were met with rejection in great numbers. Black enlistments were openly discouraged after the four Regular Army Regiments were brought up to full strength. In an Associated Press Telegram from Richmond, Virginia dated April 24th, 1917, the following edict was declared, "no more Negroes will be accepted for enlistment in the U.S. Army at present." Attesting to this is the personal account of one such patriot. Austin M. Roberts of Columbus, Ohio was denied the opportunity to volunteer for military service. In his words, he was, "unable to enlist as no colored were being accepted for a time."[9] He was later drafted into the Army.

Notwithstanding this edict, the Administration realized it needed the service of all Americans in much greater numbers than the current force. Drastic measures were in order to meet the demand. The Selective Service Act of May 1917 provided the solution. The Act granted the President the power to raise a fighting force by conscription. This was the first act mandating American military service since the Civil War. It required that all able bodied men from the ages of twenty-one to thirty (later adjusted to eighteen through forty-five), had to register for the draft, regardless of race.

The Selective Service Act opened the door for black Americans to serve and contribute to the high ideals of freedom, democracy, equality and justice. This Act would provide equal opportunity for all Americans, regardless of race, to serve the nation. Or, would it?

As America entered World War I, an age-old conflict that dated back to the origin of our great nation was again encountered. Black Americans would grapple with the opposing realities of their struggle for equality, and their patriotic duty to the nation. In the early-1900s the experiences of inequality, and injustice seemed endless. Some fifty-four years since the Emancipation Proclamation, the wounds and images of slavery were still vivid and full citizenship not yet realized. The social gains achieved since the Civil War had been systematically diminished. Just nineteen years removed from the gallant charge of black Americans at San Juan Hill, the quality, capabilities, bravery, and patriotism of black Americans were still the argument of the day, and Jim Crow was the law of the land. To further exacerbate the problem, pro-German propagandists exploited theses conditions in vigorous attempts to "dampen the ardor and cool the patriotism of African-Americans"[10], and increase tension, suspicion and unrest between black and white Americans.

At the beginning, the War Department was uncertain as to just exactly what attitude it should adopt with regards to enlisting and training black men. When America declared war against Imperial Germany, President Wilson, whose administration, was a product of the times and held polices regarding the races that reflected Jim Crow, knew he needed the service and cooperation of black Americans to successfully prosecute the war. The debates centered on the role of black men in the contest. There were points of view that discouraged the training and use of Negroes in combat units. Southerners especially, raised the age-old fear of armed black men trained to fight, and saw this prospect as a threat against their way of life. Others questioned their bravery and loyalty to the nation.

Some impugned their intellectual capacity to serve as officers, or in certain military occupational specialties. Emmett J. Scott, Special Assistant to Secretary of War Newton Baker, admitted, "it seemed difficult to convince certain subordinate members of the Secretary's staff that Negro men possessed the mentality and college training considered as a necessary prerequisite to being trained as Field Artillery officers.[11]" The Administration initially saw no role for black Americans as a viable fighting force. In concert with this, the War Department had no intention to employ black soldiers as combat troops. Instead they were planned for service as labor troops…ditch diggers, cooks, stevedores, and the like. Early pressure from the "Negro press" and activist leaders were met with ambivalence. In response to growing protests against the War Department's position, Secretary Baker responded on December 4th 1917 with this explanation; "… as you know, it has been my policy to discourage discrimination … at the same time, there is no intention on the part of the War Department to undertake at this time to settle the so-called race question … there is a need for both white and colored men alike … some must fight in the trenches, while others must serve in other capacities behind the firing lines." The Secretary further explained that white officers have been and will continue to be assigned to Service Battalions. Secretary Baker's response to what he called the "over-worked hysteria" by some complainants was widely seen as intent by the War Department to continue the longtime assignment practices limiting black Americans to non-combat roles. Some of those with firsthand experience with the bravery and fighting spirit of black combat troops were also products of their time. For example, the public and private remarks of General Pershing, Commander of the American Expeditionary Forces (AEF) in Europe, often reflected conflicting attitudes. In a secret communiqué concerning colored troops sent to the French military stationed with the American Army dated August 7, 1918, he writes, "We must not eat with them, must not shake hands with them, seek to talk to them or to meet with them outside the requirements of military service. We must not commend too highly these troops, especially in front of white Americans …" Yet his public pronouncements reflected great respect and admiration for black combat troops. He often spoke very highly of his service with the 10th U.S. Cavalry, referring to them as "gallant with zealous devotion to duty." In spite of these attitudes, black Americans responded in great numbers, eager to do their part. Yes, some were motivated by potential economic gain, some were motivated by potential social gain, most were motivated by a patriotic spirit, but they all served the country, contributing to something greater than themselves with lasting benefits for generations.

The Selective Service Act notwithstanding, the environment for military service as combat troops was tenuous at best: the already existing, combat tested and combat proven 24th and 25th Infantry and the 9th and 10th Cavalry Regiments would remain on duty in the American west and the Philippines. The highest-ranking colored officer on active duty was Lieutenant Colonel Charles Young who was suddenly declared physically unfit for continued service and summarily retired. To further exasperate the social climate, there were seventy black men lynched without trial in 1917. Nonetheless, black leaders continued to encourage service in the armed forces and demand that black soldiers be used as combat troops. Regardless of the long list of reasons why black Americans should not serve a nation that did not embrace them, they were encouraged by the likes of Dr. W.E.B. DuBois to "swallow their bitterness and enlist in the military." Many black American leaders viewed military service as a vehicle through which full participation in American society could be achieved. The NAACP, in their newsletter; The Crisis, declared: " ... first your Country, then your Rights!" So, with the regular colored troops sidelined, and considerable pressure from civil rights activists, the War Department drew from the National Guard regiments, various separate companies and black civilian draftees to create two Infantry Divisions, the 92nd and 93rd.

While many influences were brought to bear upon black Americans to entice them to evade their duty to their country and legitimate reasons why the black man should not serve in World War I were in profusion, they did not succumb to these circumstances. Instead, as in past wars, they chose to serve. Courageous and committed service was rendered. Great contributions offered, and history – American history – was made by these *Willing Patriots.*

Robert J. Dalessandro and Gerald Torrence
Carlisle, Pennsylvania 2008.

• • •

Authors note: Throughout this work we chose to use the original language of the period. As an example, the modern reader will find many of the Signal Corps photographic captions offensive. We felt that changing World War I period text so as not to offend the modern reader would be a disservice to these patriots.

As you read this volume, you will begin to understand what these civil rights pioneers faced as they strove to serve their country. Finally, chose to include the heretofore unpublished Army War College report "The use of Negro Manpower in War." We felt that the shortsightedness and inability of the Army to rise above racial prejudice was a sad reminder of the outcome of these men's efforts in World War I.

Many visionaries had hoped that service in the Army for Black Americans would signal the end of segregation and racial intolerance in America. Despite their noble efforts, America would wait decades to see that promise fulfilled. As you look into the faces of these young men, remember them as social pioneers and the great Americans that they were.

RJD and GT

Abbreviations

BHD	*Brief Histories of Divisions, U.S. Army 1917-1918,* 1921.
AABE	*American Armies and Battlefields in Europe,* 1938.
OB	*Order of Battle of the United States Land Forces in the World War,* 1931.
Castelbled	*History of the AEF,* 1937.
Farrow	*A Dictionary of military Terms,* 1918.
OAEF	*United States Army in the World War, 1917-1919, Organization of the American Expeditionary Forces,* 1988.
BPOAEF	*Battle Participation of Organizations of the American Expeditionary Forces in France, Belgium and Italy 1917-1918,* 1920.
Wilson	*Armies, Corps, Divisions, and Separate Brigades,* 1993.
JBW	*Maneuver and Firepower The Evolution of Divisions and Separate Brigades,* 1998.

CHAPTER ONE

SUPPORT TROOPS FOR THE AMERICAN EXPEDITIONARY FORCES:
COLORED ORGANIZATIONS IN THE SERVICES OF SUPPLY, ARMIES AND CORPS

Services of Supply[1]

The preponderance of black units and soldiers would ultimately be assigned to the Services of Supply. Emmett Scott stated, "To the Negro soldiers of the American Army fell a large part of the work of this "Service of Supply," or as it is known in Army slang, the "S.O.S." The work of the Negro Stevedore Regiments and Labor Battalions, and their unremitting toil at the French Ports – Brest, St. Nazaire, Bordeaux, Havre, Marseilles – won the highest praise from all who had the opportunity to judge the efficiency of their work."[2] The Services of Supply employed a variety of black units including Pioneer Infantry, Stevedore Regiments, Engineer and Labor Battalions. Additional units were assigned fulfilling functions ranging from motor transport to laundry, butchery and food preparation.

The Services of Supply was created by the Army Field Service Regulation. The primary mission was to relieve the combat forces, "from every consideration except that of defeating the enemy." As such, it was responsible for running the Lines of Communication and most all of the activities in support of the AEF combat forces in the field. Geographically it included all of France and Great Britain. It was divided into seven Base Sections, an Intermediate Section, an Advanced Section, and two independent Districts, Paris and Tours. In October 1918, an additional base section was organized to administer to troops in Italy and in 1919 a base section was established to support the Army of Occupation. The headquarters was at Tours.[3]

Below: Major General Francis J. Kernan, Commanding General of the Services of Supply. Courtesy National Archives

Bottom right: Chateau Beaulieu, Major General Kernan's residence in Tours, France, July, 1918. Major General Kernan is standing in the foreground. Courtesy National Archives

Commanding Generals

Colonel David S. Stanley (Ad interim), Major General Richard S. Blanchard, Brigadier General Mason M. Patrick (Ad interim), Major General Francis J. Kernan, and Major General James G. Harbold.

Insignia

Services of Supply

The Service of Supply selected a monogram of "SOS" of red on a blue background. Variations are known where the colors are reversed. Many of the subordinate activities of the Service of Supply created individual patches. Examples are known to exist for units down to detachment level.

The advance section of the Services of Supply was located in the north and northeastern part of France, and embraced in a general way the territory north of Paris, and Dijon. Its geographical limits, as prescribed by General Orders, No.75, Headquarters, A.E.F., December 14, 1917, included the Departments of Nord, Pas du Calais, Somme, Oise, Aisne, Ardennes, Marne, Merthe et Moselle, Meuse, Haute Marne, Cote d'Or, Vosges, Haute Saone, and Doubs. These limits were somewhat changed from time to time.

This section, which was that immediately behind the front, contained twenty-two training areas where tactical divisions were billeted, either on their way to the front or for rest, replacement, or refitting. In addition to these were the training areas where troops were trained, the staff and line schools of all branches of the service, the supply depots, and other installations of the technical services. Despite the fact that practically all of these areas and formations were under direct control of either general headquarters of the American Expeditionary Forces, or Headquarters, Services of Supply, the number of troops under the jurisdiction of the section commander sometimes amounted to more than 200,000. The section had been organized to extend the jurisdiction of the commanding officer, Services of Supply, up to the points where supplies would be delivered to the field transportation of combat forces, but in practice distribution was made from regulating stations which were under the direct control of the general staff, general headquarters. Headquarters of the advance section were located at Neufchateau, opened on November 1, 1917.

Commanders of the Advance Section were Lieutenant Colonel John F. Madden, Colonel Harry Burgess, Colonel Johnson Hagood, Brigadier General William R. Sample, and Colonel John S. Switzer.

Crude felt on felt SOS insignia.

Standard die cut felt on felt version of the SOS insignia.

The version features unusual reversed colors.

Embroidered on felt SOS monogram.

Advanced Section Services of Supply of embroidered on wool construction.

This example is embroidered in only one color.

Insignia

Advanced Section

The insignia of the Advanced Section consisted of a red Cross of Lorraine upon a blue bordered grey or olive drab disc flanked by the letter "A" and "S" in red. Photographic evidence strongly shows this insignia to be the most common device encountered on the uniforms of black soldier.

Principal Stations and Depots of the Advanced Section

Name	Established	Activities
Dijon (Côte-d'Or)	July 26, 1917	QM Depot
Jonchery(Haute-Marne)	Oct. 25, 1917	Ordnance Depot
Is-sur-Tille (Côte-d'Or)	Sept 20, 1917	Regulating Station
Neufchâteau (Vosges)	Nov. 2, 1917	HQ, Advance Section
Bourbonne-les-Bains (Haute-Marne)	Nov. 8, 1917	Remount
Colombey-les-Belles (Meurthe-et-Moselle)	Nov. 13, 1917	Air Service Depot
Eclaron (Haute-Marne)	Dec. 22, 1917	Forestry
Vittel (Vosges)	Jan. 27, 1918	Hospital Center
Langres (Haute-Marne)	Feb 4, 1918	Motor Transport
Bricon (Haute-Marne)	Apr. 3, 1918	Forestry
Poincon (Seine-Inférieure)	May 10, 1918	Chemical Warfare Svc Depot
Bazoilles (Vosges)	July 2, 1918	(Hospital Center)
Doulaincourt (Haute-Marne)	July 12, 1918	Ordnance Repair Shop
Beaune (Côte-d'Or)	July 31, 1918	Hospital Center
Lux (Côte-d'Or)	July 1918	Remount
Toul (Meurthe-et-Moselle)	Aug. 27, 1918	Hospital Center
St-Dizier (Haute-Marne)	Sept. 2, 1918	Regulating Station
Rimaucourt (Haute-Marne)	Sept. 14, 1918	Hospital Center
Liffol-le-Grand (Vosges)	Oct. 12, 1918	Regulating Station

Die cut with chain stitched "AS" monogram.

Reversed construction Advanced Section insignia.

Intermediate Section, Services of Supply

This was the largest of the SOS sections situated between the Advanced and Base sections and served as a clearinghouse to accommodate traffic between the base ports and the front. The commanders of the Intermediate Section were: Lieutenant Colonel John F. Madden, Major William Elliott, Brigadier General Arthur Johnson, Brigadier General Charles Gerhardt, Major General William H. Hay, Colonel Samuel Reber, and Colonel Howard G. Davids.

Insignia

Intermediate Section

The insignia of the Intermediate Section is rarely encountered. Examples do exist of a modified Advanced Section insignia of a red Cross of Lorraine upon a blue bordered gray or olive drab disc flanked by the letter "I" and "S" in red in lieu of the "A" and "S" of Advance Section.

Very unusual hand embroidered on wool Intermediate Section insignia.

Principal Stations and Depots

Name	Established	Activities
Nevers (Nièvre)	July 10, 1917	Quartermaster Depot
Gièvres (Loir-et-Cher)	Aug 1917	General Storage Depot
Châteauroux (Indre)	Sept 1917	Base Hospital
Issoudun (Indre)	Sept 1, 1917	Quartermaster Depot
Clermont-Ferrand (Puy-de-Dôme)	Nov 1917	Aviation Instruction Center
Romorantin (Loir-et-Cher)	Jan 17, 1918	Air Svc Production Center
Blois (Loir-et-Cher)	Jan 20, 1918	Casual Officers Depot
Mehun-sur-Yèvre (Cher)	Jan 28, 1918	Ordnance Depot and Repair Shops
St-Aignan (Loir-et-Cher)	Jan 1918	Replacement Depot
Montierchaume (Indre)	Apr 1918	General Storage Depot
Orléans (Loiret)	June 1918	Base Hospital
Mesves-sur-Loire (Nièvre)	June 15, 1918	Hospital Center
Allerey (Saône-et-Loire)	June 23, 1918	Hospital Center
Verneuil (Nièvre)	July 14, 1918	Motor Reconstruction
Mars-sur-Allier (Nièvre)	July 19, 1918	Hospital Center
Sougy (Nièvre)	Aug 1, 1918	Veterinary Hospital
Le Mans (Sarthe)	Aug 1, 1918	Replacement Depot
Vichy (Allier)	Aug 12, 1918	Hospital Center
Lyon (Rhone)	Aug 19, 1918	Salvage Depot
Chenevières (Meurthe-et-Moselle)	Sept 9, 1918	Ordnance Depot
Le Mans (Sarthe)	Dec 15, 1918	Embarkation Center

Base Section #1
Principal Stations and Depots

Name	Established	Activities
St-Nazaire (Loire-Inférieure)	June 22, 1917	Base Port
Nantes (Loire-Inférieure)	July 11, 1917	Base Port
Savenay (Loire-Inférieure)	Aug 21, 1917	Base Hospital
Les Sables d'Olonne (Vendée)	Aug 31, 1917	Base Port
Saumur (Maine-et-Loire)	Sept 6, 1917	Artillery School
Coëtquidan (Morbihan)	Sept 27, 1917	Arty Camp/Aerial Observation School

Angers (Maine-et-Loir)	Oct 19, 1917	Engineers Training Base
Paimboeuf (Loire-Inférieure)	Nov 30, 1917	Naval Air Station
St-Maxient (Deux-Sèvres)	Dec 9, 1918	Air Service Replacement
Fromentine (Vendée)	Feb 4, 1918	Naval Air Station
La Trinité-Porhoët (Morbihan)	Mar 14, 1918	Naval Air Station
Meucon (Morbihan)	Apr 14, 1918	Artillery Camp
St-Jean-de-Monts (Vendée)	May 7, 1918	Air Gunnery School

Base Section #2
Principal Stations and Depots

Name	Established	Activities
Talence (Gironde)	July 28, 1917	Base Hospital
Bordeaux (Gironde)	Aug 30, 1917	Base Port
Grange-Neuve (Gironde)	Sept 1, 1917	Rest and Embarkation
Génicart (Gironde)	Sept 1, 1917	Rest and Embarkation
Bassens Dock (Gironde)	Nov 2, 1917	Freight debarkation
Camp de Souge (Gironde)	Nov 11, 1917	Artillery training
Merignac (Gironde)	Nov 1917	Remount depot
Dax (Landes)	Dec 22, 1917	Forestry Hospital
Limoges (Haute Vienne)	Jan 1, 1918	Hospitals/artillery training
Mimizan (Landes)	Jan 19, 1918	Forestry
Libourne (Gironde)	Feb 9, 1918	O & T Center
Cazaux (Ariège)	Feb 9, 1918	Air Instruction Center
Le Courneau (Gironde) Camp Hunt	Feb 19, 1918	Artillery training
La Courtine (Creuse)	Feb 1918	Artillery training
Montpont (Saône-et-Loire)	Mar 3, 1918	Base Hospital
Carbon Blanc (Gironde)	Apr 18, 1918	Remount
St-Supplylice (Gironde)	Apr 21, 1918	Storage Depot
Beau Desert (Gironde)	June 22, 1918	Hospital Center
Bayonne (Basses Pyrénées)	Aug 15, 1918	Remount
Perigueux (Dordogne)	Sept 5, 1918	Hospitals
St-Loubes (Gironde)	Sept 12, 1918	Ammunition depot
Angouléme (Charente)	Sept 1918	O & T Center

Base Section #3
Principal Stations and Depots

Name	Established	Activities
Southampton, England	Sept 1, 1917	Rest Camp
Winchester, England	Nov 7, 1917	Rest Camp
Romsey, England	Dec 26, 1917	Rest Camp
London Depot, England	Dec 1917	Transit Depot
Paignton, England	Jan 1, 1918	Hospital
Liverpool, England	Jan 10, 1918	Hospital
Hursley Park, England	Apr 20, 1918	Hospital
Knotty Ash, England	Apr 24, 1918	Rest Camp
Flower Down, England	July 26, 1918	Air Service Camp
Swansea Depot, Wales	June 1918	Storage Depot
Dartford, England	July 18, 1918	Hospital
Portsmouth, England	July 28, 1918	Hospital
Tottenham, England	Aug 1, 1918	Hospital
Codford, England	Sept 23, 1918	Air Service Camp
Sarisbury Court	Sept 27, 1918	Hospital

Base Section #4
Principal Stations and Depots

Name	Established	Activities
Rouen (Seine-Inférieure)	May 25, 1917	Sub-Base
Boulogne (Pas-de-Calais)	May 30, 1917	Hospital
Etretat (Seine-Inférieure)	May 31, 1917	Hospital
Dannes-Camiers (Pas-de-Calais)	June 11, 1917	Hospital
Le Tréport (Seine-Inférieure)	June 12, 1917	Hospital
Le Havre (Seine-Inférieure)	Aug 2, 1917	Base Port
Calais (Pas-de-Calais)	June 28, 1918	Sub-Base
Caen (Calvados)	Sept 15, 1918	Hospital
Dunkirk (Nord)	Dec 10, 1918	Hospital

Base Section #5
Principal Stations and Depots

Name	Established	Activities
Rennes (Ille-et-Vilaine)	Sept 7, 1917	Railroad operation
Brest (Finistère)	Nov 10, 1917	Base Port
Pontanezen (Finistère)	Jan 1918	Rest and Embarkation
Landerneau (Finistère)	June 1, 1918	Hospital
Cherbourg (Manche)	June 25, 1918	Port
St-Malo (Ill-et-Vilaine)	Aug 18, 1918	Leave area
Kerhornou (Finistère)	Sept 16, 1918	Hospital center
Granville (Manche)	Oct 12, 1918	Coal Port

Base Section #6
Principal Stations and Depots

Name	Established	Activities
Marseille (Bouches-du-Rhône)	May 30, 1918	Base Port
Marseille (Bouches-du-Rhône)	June 21, 1918	Motor Reception Park
Miramas (Bouches-du-Rhône)	July 9, 1918	Storage Depot
"Riviera" (Alpes-Maritimes)	July 1918	Hospital Center
Toulon (Var)	Aug 25, 1918	Port

Base Section #7
Principal Stations and Depots

Name	Established	Activities
La Pallice (Charente-Inférieure)	Nov 7, 1917	Base Port
La Rochelle (Charente-Inférieure)	Jan 17, 1918	Camp Pullman
Rochefort-sur-Mer (Charente-Inférieure)	Jan 26, 1918	Port
Pèrigny (Charente-Inférieure)	Mar 1, 1918	Hospital
Tonnay-Charente (Charente-Inférieure)	June 20, 1918	Coal Port
Mortagne-sur-Girond (Charente-Inférieure)	July 17, 1918	Cement Mill
Marans (Charente-Inférieure)	Aug 13, 1918	Port
Aytre (Charente-Inférieure)	Oct 1, 1918	Car Erecting Plant
Aigrefeuille-d'Aunis (Charente-Inférieure)	Oct 11, 1918	Hospital

Base Section #8
Principal Stations and Depots

Name	Established	Activities
Foggia, Italy	Sept 28, 1917	Aerial Training
Furbara, Italy	May 13, 1918	Aerial Gunnery
Genoa, Italy	June 14, 1918	Port
Mantua, Italy	July 19, 1918	Motor Transport Corps Shop
Villafranca di Verona, Italy	July 26, 1918	Infantry Camp
Castelfranco, Italy	Sept 7, 1918	Motor Transport Corps Shop
Vicenza, Italy	Sept 7, 1918	Hospital
Padua, Italy	Oct 28, 1918	American Red Cross Hospital
Alessandria, Italy	Oct 31, 1918	Supply Dept

Base Section #9
Principal Stations and Depots

Name	Established	Activities
Rotterdam (Holland)	Mar 1, 1919	Sub-Base
Antwerp (Belgium)	Mar 22, 1919	Base Port

District of Paris

The District of Paris was responsible for activities within the environs of the city of Paris.

Principal Stations and Depots

Name	Established	Activities
Neuilly-sur-Seine (Seine)	July 23, 1917	Hospital
Paris (Seine)	Nov 1, 1917	Hospital
Paris (Seine)	Nov 15, 1917	Hospital
Joinville-le-Pont (Seine)	Apr 26, 1918	Hospital
Auteuil (Seine-et-Oise)	May 27, 1918	Hospital
Paris (Seine)	June 6, 1918	Engineer Depot
Aubervilliers (Seine)	June 13, 1918	Medical Supply Depot
Paris (Seine)	June 27, 1918	Overhaul Park
Paris (Seine)	July 20, 1918	Hospital
St Denis (Seine)	July 25, 1918	Hospital
Sèvres (Seine-et-Oise)	Aug 6, 1918	Hospital
St Cloud (Seine-et-Oise)	Sept 14, 1918	Convalescent Home
Paris (Seine)	Sept 16, 1918	Hospital
Paris (Seine)	Sept 26, 1918	Hospital
Nogent-sur-Marne (Seine)	Nov 1, 1918	Convalescent Camp

Colored units Serving in the Services of Supply

Engineers

All of the Colored Engineer organizations were designated as "Colored Service Battalions" and were formally numbered in the 500 series starting with the 506th Engineer Battalion and running through the 567th Engineer Battalion. Some of the numbered battalions were authorized but not raised, so gaps exist numerically in the series. AEF Headquarters assigned these battalions to both the SOS and the numbered Armies. Engineer Service Battalions consisted of a Headquarters Detachment, four companies and a Medical Department with an aggregate strength of 1,040 men. Each

This group of soldiers wears a hodge-podge of American and British uniform items; the soldier seated in the center appears to be wearing an Engineer collar disk on his overseas cap. Courtesy Private Collection.

of the companies had three officers and 250 soldiers and was equipped with one 1/2 ton motor truck, two two-ton motor trucks, a water cart and two motorcycles with sidecar and was designed to accomplish a variety of labor related tasks including bridging, road construction/repair, and other general engineering tasks.[4] There seems to be little difference between the efforts of colored Engineers and the Pioneer Infantry Regiments in France. However, the non-commissioned officers of the Pioneer Infantry Regiments were often colored, and in many regiments, they retained their arms. Conversely, the colored Engineers rarely advanced beyond the rank of corporal, and although they were trained in the use of firearms in the United States, for the most part, they were not permitted to carry them in France. A corporal of the 546th Engineers wrote, "Although some of us worked quite close behind the lines, within range of shot and shell, we did not see arms except such as lay discarded about the woods and in the fields."[5]

Units[6]

506th Engineer Service Battalion. The battalion was organized in October 1917 at Camp Lee, Virginia and it sailed for France from Hoboken, New Jersey in January 1918. The unit served with the SOS until May 1919 when it returned to Camp Merritt, New Jersey and was demobilized the same month at Camp Meade, Maryland.

507th Engineer Service Battalion. The battalion was organized in November 1917 at Camp Travis, Texas, and it sailed for France from Hoboken, New Jersey in February 1918 it was absorbed by the 20th Engineer Regiment and served with the SOS until demobilization at Camp Merritt, New Jersey in May 1919.

509th Engineer Service Battalion. The battalion was organized in October 1917 at Camp Travis, Texas, and it sailed for France from Hoboken, New Jersey in February 1918. The unit served with the SOS until June 1919 when it returned to Camp Upton, New York and was demobilized the same month at Camp Travis, Texas.

510th Engineer Service Battalion. The battalion was organized in January 1918 at Camp Lee, Virginia, and it sailed for France from Hoboken, New Jersey in March 1918. The unit served with the SOS. Companies A and B and the Medical Detachment were ordered to Base Section Number 1, St. Nazaire, Company C to Jonchery and Company D to Liffol-le Grand. In April, two officers and fifteen men were transferred to New Kent, England where they were assigned to work the cement mills at Swanscomabe. Company C was transferred to Camp Montierchaume in August. In June 1919 when it returned to Camp Upton, New York and was demobilized the same month at Camp Lee, Virginia.[7]

511th Engineer Service Battalion. The battalion was organized in January 1918 at Camp Lee, Virginia, and it sailed for France from Hoboken, New Jersey in March 1918. The unit served with the SOS until June 1919 when it returned to Camp Alexander, Virginia and was demobilized the same month at Camp Lee, Virginia.

512th Engineer Service Battalion. The battalion was organized in January 1918 at Camp Pike, Arkansas, and it sailed for France from Hoboken, New Jersey in April 1918. The unit served with the SOS until June 1919 when it returned to Camp Upton, New York and was demobilized the same month at Camp Pike, Arkansas.

514th Engineer Service Battalion. The battalion was organized in February 1918 at Camp Gordon, Georgia, and it sailed for France from Newport News, Virginia in April 1918. The unit served with the SOS until June 1919 when it returned to Camp Upton, New York and was demobilized the same month at Camp Gordon, Georgia

515th Engineer Service Battalion. The battalion was organized in January 1918 at Camp Zachary Taylor, Kentucky, and it sailed for France from Hoboken, New Jersey in May 1918. The unit served with the SOS until July 1919 when it returned to Camp Mills, New York and was demobilized the same month at Camp Zachary Taylor, Kentucky.

517th Engineer Service Battalion. The battalion was organized in April 1918 at Camp Gordon, Georgia, and it sailed for France from Newport News, Virginia in July 1918. It served with the SOS until it was absorbed by the 20th Engineer Regiment.

518th Engineer Service Battalion. The battalion was organized in May 1918 at Camp Gordon, Georgia, and it sailed for France from Hoboken, New Jersey in September 1918. It served with the SOS until it was converted into a Transportation Corps unit.

519th Engineer Service Battalion. The battalion was organized in April 1918 at Camp Devens, Massachusetts, and it sailed for France from Hoboken, New Jersey in July 1918. It served with the SOS until it was absorbed by the 20th Engineer Regiment in October 1918.

Opposite
Top: Company C, 524th Engineers, pulling down a shell torn building in Flirey – to mend the roads through the German trenches which were blown up before the German retreat. Flirey, Meurthe et Moselle, France. September 14, 1918. Courtesy National Archives.

Bottom: A close up of workers on the bridge across the Aire River which is being built by French and American Engineers. Boureuilles, Meuse, France. October 25, 1918.

Corporal Bob Pfeiffer, Company I, 23rd Engineers, which was composed of many consolidated Engineer Service Battalions, has discarded his helmet for a silk hat taken from the ruins of Theancourt, Moselle, France. October 24, 1918. Courtesy Private Collection.

520th Engineer Service Battalion. The battalion was organized in April 1918 at Camp Devens, Massachusetts; it was assigned to Camp A.A. Humphreys, Virginia in June 1918 and it sailed for France from Hoboken, New Jersey in August 1918. The unit served with the SOS until June 1919 when it returned to Camp Alexander, Virginia and was demobilized at Camp Sherman, Ohio in July 1919.

521st Engineer Service Battalion. The battalion was organized in April 1918 at Camp Meade, Maryland; it was assigned to Camp A.A. Humphreys, Virginia in the same month. It sailed for France from Hoboken, New Jersey in August1918. The unit served with the SOS until June 1919 when it returned to Camp Jackson, South Carolina and was demobilized.

523rd Engineer Service Battalion. The battalion was organized in March 1918 at Camp Pike, Arkansas it was transferred to Camp A.A. Humphreys, Virginia in May 1918 and then to Camp Stuart, Virginia in June 1918. The battalion sailed for France from Newport News, Virginia in July 1918. It served with the SOS until it was absorbed by the 20th Engineer Regiment in October 1918.

525th Engineer Service Battalion. The battalion was organized in April 1918 at Camp Pike, Arkansas it was transferred to Camp A.A. Humphreys, Virginia in May 1918 and then to Camp Stuart, Virginia in June 1918. The battalion sailed for France from Newport News, Virginia in July 1918. It served with the SOS until July 1919 when it returned to Norfolk, Virginia. It was demobilized the same month at Camp Shelby, Mississippi.

526th Engineer Service Battalion. The battalion was organized in May 1918 at Camp Pike, Arkansas. The battalion sailed for France from Newport News, Virginia in July 1918. It served with the SOS until July 1919 when it returned to Norfolk, Virginia. It was demobilized the same month at Camp Shelby, Mississippi.

531st Engineer Service Battalion. The battalion was organized in April 1918 at Camp Travis, Texas it was transferred to Camp Upton, New York in June 1918. The battalion sailed for France from Hoboken, New Jersey in June 1918. It served with the SOS until it was absorbed by the 20th Engineer Regiment in October 1918.

533rd Engineer Service Battalion. The battalion was organized in June 1918 at Camp Pike, Arkansas. It sailed for France from Hoboken, New Jersey in August 1918. It served with the SOS until it was absorbed by the 20th Engineer Regiment in October 1918.

Opposite
Top: The original Signal Corps caption reads: 508th Engineers, Company C, three prizes of Company Menil-la-Tour, France, March 14, 1918. Courtesy National Archives.

Bottom left: Sgt. Eugene E. Hoffman, Company A., 537th Engineers, holding a German trap taken from the captured trenches south of Boureuilles, Meuse, France. October 27th, 1918. Courtesy National Archives.

Bottom right: Private Jerry Walker, Company A, 537th Engineers, standing beside the stone masonry of the German trenches. South of the Boureuilles Meuse, France. October 27th, 1918. Courtesy National Archives.

Below: Colored troops of the 528th Engineers reballasting light railway. Road taken over from the French. Gormeville, Meuse, France. October 30th, 1918. Courtesy National Archives.

Above: 508th Engineers, Company C. building roads. Menil-la-Tour, France. March 14, 1918. Courtesy National Archives.

Below: Group photo of the 510th Engineer Service Regiment possibly Company C.; the reverse of the photo reads From Corporal Emmitt Franklin, Port Montierchaume, Indre, France and lists the Army Post Office Number 738. Courtesy Private Collection.

Above: The Regimental Band of the 317th Engineer Service Regiment. Courtesy Private Collection.

Below: The work of an Inland Water Transportation Company, formally 57th Engineer Regiment, another consoli-dated engineer unit. Their job is to ship supplies to troops by means of inland waterways and in that manner help relieve the railroads. On one side of the hangers the little French freight cars are being loaded; on the other, barges are being loaded, Le Havre, Seine-Inferieure. France. February 10, 1919. Courtesy National Archives.

Two engineers pose in France. The man on the left wears an Engineer Private First Class insignia on his shirtsleeve. Courtesy Private Collection.

536th Engineer Service Battalion. The battalion was organized in May 1918 at Camp Custer, Michigan, and transferred to Camp Upton, New York in August 1918. It sailed for France from Hoboken, New Jersey in August 1918. It served with the SOS until July 1919 when it returned to Camp Jackson, South Carolina and was demobilized.

538th Engineer Service Battalion. The battalion was organized in May 1918 at Camp Meade, Maryland it sailed for France from Hoboken, New Jersey in August 1918. It served with the SOS until it was converted into a Transportation Corps unit in December 1918.

540th Engineer Service Battalion. The battalion was organized in August 1918 at Camp Humphreys, Virginia. It was transferred to Camp Merritt, New Jersey in October and it sailed for France from Hoboken, New Jersey that same month. The unit served with the SOS until June 1919 when it returned to Camp Upton, New York and was demobilized in July at Camp Lee, Virginia.

545th Engineer Service Battalion. The battalion was organized in August 1918 at Camp Humphreys, Virginia. It sailed for France from Hoboken, New Jersey in September 1918. The unit served with the SOS until June 1919 when it returned to, Camp Merritt, New Jersey. The battalion was demobilized Camp Meade, Maryland later that month.

547th Engineer Service Battalion. The battalion was organized in September 1918 at Camp Humphreys, Virginia. It was transferred to Camp Merritt, New Jersey in October 1918 and sailed for France from Hoboken, New Jersey later in the month. The unit served with the SOS until June 1919 when it returned to, Newport News, Virginia; the battalion was demobilized at Camp Lee, Virginia that same month.

548th Engineer Service Battalion. The battalion was organized in September 1918 at Camp Humphreys, Virginia. It was transferred to Camp Merritt, New Jersey in October 1918 and sailed for France from Hoboken, New Jersey later in the month. The unit served with the SOS until June 1919 when it returned to, Camp Mills, New York; the battalion was demobilized at Camp Gordon, Georgia that same month.

549th Engineer Service Battalion. The battalion was organized in September 1918 at Camp Humphreys, Virginia. It was transferred to Camp Merritt, New Jersey in November 1918 and sailed for France from Hoboken, New Jersey later in the month. The unit served with the SOS until June 1919 when it returned to, Camp Alexander, Virginia; the battalion was demobilized at Camp Lee, Virginia that same month.

550th Engineer Service Battalion. The battalion was organized in September 1918 at Camp Humphreys, Virginia. It was transferred to Camp Merritt, New Jersey in November 1918 and sailed for France from Hoboken, New Jersey later in the month. The unit served with the SOS until June 1919 when it returned to, Camp Mills, New York; the battalion was demobilized at Camp Gordon, Georgia that same month.

701st Engineer Battalion (Stevedore). The battalion was organized in September 1918 at Camp Alexander, Virginia it sailed from Newport News, Virginia in October. It was converted to a Transportation Corps unit in December 1918.

701st Engineer Battalion (Stevedore). The battalion was organized in September 1918 at Camp Alexander, Virginia it sailed from Newport News, Virginia in October 1918. It was converted to a Transportation Corps unit in December 1918.

702nd Engineer Battalion (Stevedore). The battalion was organized in October 1918 at Camp Alexander, Virginia it sailed from Newport News, Virginia in November 1918. It was converted to a Transportation Corps unit in December 1918.

Pioneer Infantry[8]

A Pioneer Infantry Regiment had an aggregate strength of 3,551 men. It was composed of a headquarters and headquarters company, a supply company, three infantry battalions, a medical department and chaplains. Each battalion consisted of a headquarters and four companies. Each Pioneer infantry company consisted of six officers and 250 men. The Regiment was equipped with fourteen four-mule combat wagons, twenty four-mule ration and baggage wagons, thirty-eight bicycles and two motorcycles with sidecars. In addition to being trained as infantrymen, the unit was trained to perform routine labor tasks including roadwork, general construction, and fortification construction.[9] Because the Pioneer Infantry Regiment designations ranged from 801 to 816, they were often referred to as the "8's."[10]

Units[11]

801st Pioneer Infantry Regiment. The regiment was organized at Camp Zachary Taylor, Kentucky in September 1918 it moved to Camp Merritt, New Jersey and then sailed that month from Hoboken, New Jersey. It served as a labor unit with duty at the docks until June 1919 when it returned to Camp Alexander, Virginia and was demobilized at Camp Zachery Taylor, Kentucky that same month. The unit was commanded by Colonel G.F. Hamilton.

802nd Pioneer Infantry Regiment. Twelve hundred enlisted men of the 158th Depot Brigade formed the foundation of the 802nd Pioneer Infantry Regiment. The regiment was organized at Camp Sherman, Ohio in July 1918 it moved to Camp Mills, New York in August and then sailed that month from Hoboken, New Jersey. It served as a labor unit with railroad construction duty at Clermont until July 1919 when it returned to Camp Mills, New York and was demobilized at Camp Gordon, Georgia that same month. The unit was commanded by Lieutenant Colonel A.P. Watts.

802nd Pioneer Infantry, breaking stone to build roads so that guns can be brought up to be placed into position. Cheppy, Meuse, France. October 12, 1918. Courtesy National Archives.

Members of the 802nd Pioneer Infantry digging in showing 1st Lieutenant James P. Tierney and 2nd Lieutenant John Kiene. Between Cheppy and Varennes-en-Argonne, Meuse, France. October 30, 1918. Courtesy National Archives.

Motor Transport Corps[12]

Motor Transport Companies had an aggregate strength of eighty men (two officers and seventy-eight enlisted men) and were equipped with twenty-seven trucks.[13]

22nd Motor Truck Company. Active with the SOS in France from June 1917 until December 1919.

598th Motor Transport Company. Active with the SOS in France from October 1918 until August 1919.

Transportation Corps Stevedore

Stevedore Regiments were defined as, "Colored troops attached to the Quartermasters' department for special service."[14] These units were responsible for loading and unloading cargo at the ports.

Transportation Corps Stevedore companies were assigned to each of the five major American operated French ports (Brest, St. Nazaire, Bordeaux, Havre, and Marseilles) The companies were numbered in the 800 series. Companies assigned to the SOS in France were as follows: 801-807, 809-868. Each company had an aggregate strength of 253 (three officers and 250 enlisted men).[15]

Kitchen of 302nd Stevedore Regiment Consolidated Mess, Quartermaster Corps, Rest Camp Number 4, Bassin, France. June 10, 1918. Courtesy National Archives.

Quartette of 301st Stevedore Regiment attached to 23rd Engineers, Legney, France. May 13, 1918.

Portrait of Reese Joe Jimerson, 301st Stevedore Regiment; Jimerson noted on the photograph that, "This photograph was made in St. Nazaire, France, Christmas week 1917 in a French Studio. I was in France 18 months." Courtesy Military History Institute.

Reese J. Jimerson sent this picture of himself and one of his prize garden vegetables to Military History Institute when he returned his veteran's survey in the 1970s. Courtesy Military History Institute.

Jimerson penned these remarks on a view of the busy Port of St. Nazaire where the 301st Stevedore Regiment was assigned. St. Nazaire was one of the principal American run ports supporting the American Expeditionary Forces. Courtesy Military History Institute.

Another view of the Port of St. Nazaire, France. Courtesy Military History Institute.

Below: The Regimental Band of the 301st Stevedore Regiment at Camp Number 4, St. Nazaire, France. Note the two soldiers looking out from behind the window at right.

Right: Interior of kitchen, Sorting Yard Mess Stevedores, Transportation Corps Base Section Number 5, Brest, Finistare, France. October 29, 1918. Courtesy National Archives.

Below: 804th Stevedore Battalion Band at Camp Number 4, St. Nazaire, Loire-Inferieure, France. Base Section Number 1, November 1, 1918. Courtesy National Archives.

Bottom: Sergeant Montague (on left) and mess crew; Base Section Number 5. Brest, Finistere, France. October 29, 1918. Courtesy National Archives.

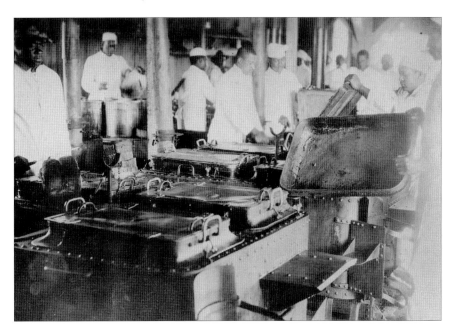

Leonard Carroll and Frank S. Clay, 10th Company, 302nd Stevedore Regiment pose together in France. Note the Mechanic insignia worn by Carroll. Courtesy Private Collection.

Above: Sergeant Montague lining up his boys. Transportation Corps, Base Section Number 5. Brest, Finistere, France, October 29, 1918. Courtesy National Archives.

Below: The docks at St. Nazaire from the deck of the U.S.S. Arizona, June 1919. The soldiers waiting to embark are black troops. Courtesy Private Collection.

Colored YMCA at St. Nazaire, France. Courtesy National Archives.

This unknown group of soldiers (likely Transportation Corps drivers) wear Mackinaw coats and M-1907 winter "drivers" caps backward. It is our belief based on examination of many other images that the photographer told these soldiers to reverse the caps to reduce shadows on their faces due to darker skin tone. Courtesy Private Collection.

Quartermaster Corps[16]
333rd Bakery Company. Active with the SOS from August 1917 until March 1919. The Bakery Company had an aggregate strength of 103 men (two officers and 101 enlisted men).[17]

383rd Bakery Company. Active with the SOS May 1918 until March 1919.

322nd Butchery Company. Active in France from July 1918 until August 1919. A Butchery Company had an aggregate strength of fifty-seven men (one Officer and fifty-six enlisted men).[18]

Service (Labor) Battalions[19]
A Service Battalion had an aggregate strength of 1,248 with seventeen white officers, forty-eight white soldiers and 1,183 black soldiers. It consisted of a headquarters, four companies and a medical department. The unit was equipped with two motor trucks, one water cart and two motorcycles per company.[20] Farrow defined Labor Companies as "Colored troops attached to the Quartermasters' Department for special services."[21] These units were used for a variety of labor needs by the Army.

301st – 303rd Service Battalions. Never organized.

304th Service Battalion. The battalion was organized in June 1918 in France in June 1919 it returned to Camp Lee, Virginia where it was demobilized the same month.

305th Service Battalion. The battalion was organized in June 1918 in France serving with the SOS. In July 1919, it returned to Camp Mills, New York and was demobilized that same month at Camp Jackson, South Jackson, South Carolina.

306th Service Battalion. The battalion was organized in June 1918 in France serving with the SOS. In July 1919, it returned to Camp Hill, Virginia and was demobilized that same month.

307th Service Battalion. The battalion was organized in June 1918 in France serving with the SOS. In May 1919, it returned to Camp Upton, New York and was demobilized in June 1919.

Body wrapped in blanket before being placed in coffin in France, Quartermaster Corps Graves Registration Service. Courtesy National Archives.

Left: Dining car chefs aboard Hospital Train Number 54, Horreville, France April 26, 1918. Courtesy National Archives.

Right: 301st Labor Battalion, unloading wheat from lighters, Brest, France, May 7, 1918. Courtesy National Archives.

308th Service Battalion. The battalion was organized in March 1918 at Camp Hill, Virginia it moved to Newport News, Virginia in March 1918 serving with the SOS until returning to Camp Mills, New York in July 1919. It was demobilized at Camp Gordon, Georgia that month.

309th Service Battalion (4th Provisional Labor Battalion). The battalion was organized in March 1918 at Camp Hill, Virginia it moved to Newport News, Virginia in April 1918 serving with the SOS until June 1919 when it is returned to Camp Jackson, South Carolina. The unit demobilized July 1919 at Camp Pike, Arkansas.

310th Service Battalion (5th Provisional Labor Battalion). The battalion was organized in March 1918 at Camp Hill, Virginia it moved to Newport News, Virginia in April 1918 serving with the SOS until returning to Camp Jackson, South Carolina in June 1919. It was demobilized at Camp Pike, Arkansas in July 1919.

311th Service Battalion (6th Provisional Labor Battalion). The battalion was organized in March 1918 at Camp Hill, Virginia it moved to Newport News, Virginia in July 1918 serving with the SOS until returning to Camp Merritt, New Jersey in August 1919. It was demobilized at Camp Shelby, Mississippi in September 1919.

312th Service Battalion (1st Provisional Labor Battalion). The battalion was organized in March 1918 at Camp Hill, Virginia it moved to Hoboken, New Jersey in March 1918 serving with the SOS until June 1919 and returned to Camp Upton, New York. It was moved to Camp Gordon, Georgia and demobilized that same month.

313th Service Battalion (2nd Provisional Labor Battalion). The battalion was organized in March 1918 at Camp Hill, Virginia it moved to Newport News, Virginia in March 1918 serving with the SOS until June 1919 when it returned to Camp Alexander, Virginia. It was demobilized at Camp Gordon, Georgia in July 1919.

314th Service Battalion. The battalion was organized in July 1918 at Camp Gordon, Georgia it moved to Newport News, Virginia in July 1918 serving with the

Left: Unloading ship's cargo from hold on to docks. Dock Number 9, Base Section Number 2, Bassens Docks, Bordeaux, Gironde, France. November 1, 1918. Courtesy National Archives.

Right: Unloading Pig Iron in St. Nazaire. Courtesy National Archives.

SOS until July 1919 when it returned to Camp Stuart, Virginia. It was demobilized at Camp Gordon, Georgia in July 1919.

315th Service Battalion. The battalion was organized in August 1918 at Camp Gordon, Georgia it moved to Hoboken, New Jersey in September 1918 serving with the SOS until July 1919 when it returned to Camp Hill, Virginia. It was demobilized at Camp Gordon, Georgia in July 1919.

316th Service Battalion. The battalion was organized in May 1918 at Camp Joseph E. Johnston, Florida it moved to Camp Mills, New York in June 1918 where it is inactivated. Personnel from the unit were used to form both the 427th Reserve Labor Battalion and a second 316th Service Battalion. The second 316th Service Battalion was reactivated in September 1918 at Camp Alexander, Virginia. It moved to Newport News, Virginia and shipped to France in September 1918 serving with the SOS until July 1919 when it returned to Norfolk, Virginia. It was demobilized at Camp Gordon, Georgia in August 1919.

317th Service Battalion. The battalion was organized in May 1918 at Camp Zachary Taylor, Kentucky it moved to Newport News, Virginia in June 1918 and sailed for France. It served with the SOS until June 1919 when it returned to Camp Alexander, Virginia. It was demobilized at Camp Zachary Taylor, Kentucky in July 1919.

Left: View of automatic transportation tractor, used on the docks at Bassens, Gironde, France. December 13, 1918. Courtesy National Archives.

Right: Loading a car with rations, Central Medical Department Laboratory. Dijon, France. September 2, 1918. Courtesy National Archives.

Below: The original Signal Corps caption reads: The happy blacks with a little coloring, singing "Waiting at the Station 'till the Train Comes Along." Their favorite. Gievres, Nievre, France, December 2, 1918. Courtesy National Archives.

318th Service Battalion. The battalion was organized in June 1918 at Camp Hill, Virginia it moved to Newport News, Virginia in June 1918 and sailed for France. It served with the SOS until June 1919 when it returned to Camp Merritt, New Jersey. It was demobilized at Camp Shelby, Mississippi in July 1919.

319th Service Battalion. The battalion was organized in June 1918 at Camp Hill, Virginia it moved to Newport News, Virginia in July 1918 and sailed for France. It served with the SOS until July 1919 when it returned to Camp Alexander, Virginia. It was demobilized at Camp Shelby, Mississippi in July 1919.

320th Service Battalion. The battalion was organized in June 1918 at Camp Lee, Virginia it moved to Newport News, Virginia in July 1918 and sailed for France. It served with the SOS until July 1919 when it returned to Camp Alexander, Virginia. It was demobilized at Camp Lee, Virginia in July 1919.

321st Service Battalion. The battalion was organized in May 1918 at Camp Jackson, South Carolina it moved to Camp Sevier, South Carolina. In July 1918 it moved to Camp Upton, New York and sailed for France from Hoboken, New Jersey. It served with the SOS until August 1919 when it returned to Camp Merritt, New Jersey. It was demobilized at Camp Lee, Virginia in August 1919.

322nd Service Battalion. The battalion was organized in July 1918 at Camp Travis, Texas it moved to Camp Hill, Virginia in July 1918 and sailed for France in August from Newport News, Virginia. It served with the SOS until July 1919 when it returned to Camp Mills, New York. It was demobilized at Camp Travis, Texas in July 1919.

323rd Service Battalion. The battalion was organized in May 1918 at Camp Grant, Illinois it moved to Camp Upton, New York in July 1918 and sailed for France from Hoboken, New Jersey. It served with the SOS until July 1919 when it returned to Camp Mills, New York. It was demobilized at Camp Lee, Virginia in July 1919.

324th Service Battalion. The battalion was organized in July 1918 at Camp Custer, Michigan it moved to Camp Upton, New York in July 1918 and sailed for France from Hoboken, New Jersey. It served with the SOS until July 1919 when it returned to Camp Mills, New York. It was demobilized at Camp Gordon, Georgia in July 1919.

325th Service Battalion. The battalion was organized in May 1918 at Camp Funston, Kansas it moved to Camp Upton, New York in August 1918 and sailed for

Cook Evey Edward Adams was born and died in West Virginia; he stands proudly in uniform in this portrait taken in France. Courtesy Private Collection.

France from Hoboken, New Jersey. It served with the SOS until July 1919 when it returned to Camp Alexander, Virginia. It was demobilized at Camp Shelby, Mississippi in July 1919.

326th Service Battalion. The battalion was organized in September 1918 at Camp McClellan, Alabama it moved to Camp Merritt, New Jersey in October 1918 and sailed for France from Hoboken, New Jersey. It served with the SOS until June 1919 when it returned to Camp Merritt, New Jersey. It was demobilized at Camp Shelby, Mississippi in July 1919.

327th Service Battalion. The battalion was organized in June 1918 at Camp Wheeler, Georgia it moved to Camp Hill, Virginia in June 1918 and sailed for France from Newport News, Virginia. It served with the SOS until July 1919 when it returned to Camp Mills, New York. It was demobilized at Camp Gordon, Georgia in July 1919.

328th Service Battalion. The battalion was organized in March 1918 at Camp Jackson, South Carolina it moved to Pisgah Forrest, North Carolina in June 1918 where it was inactivated. It was reformed into two units: The 444th Reserve Labor Battalion was organized in October 1918 at Pisgah Forrest, North Carolina. In December 1918 it moved to Camp Sevier, South Carolina and in January 1919 demobilized at that place. The second 328th Service Battalion was organized September 1918 at Camp Alexander, Virginia and sailed for France from Newport News, Virginia in October

This French Carte Postale features a distinguished soldier wearing Quartermaster insignia on his collar. Courtesy Private Collection.

Cook (Mess Sergeant) Frank, Winfield of Bronx, New York sits for the camera in France. Courtesy Private Collection.

Right to left: Private First Class Hobart Jones, Sergeant General T. Holman and Sergeant John D. Jones pose for a photograph. The two sergeants appear to be wearing the American Ordnance Corps or French Infantry insignia on their overseas caps (a flaming bomb), Jones wears a Private First Class Cook's insignia on the right sleeve of his British Army tunic, and he also wears a British issue overseas cap. Courtesy Private Collection.

A rare view of a soldier from the 324th Labor Battalion (note the numbers "324" on overseas cap); his face shows the strain of the hard work he has performed supporting the American Expeditionary Forces. Courtesy Private Collection.

1918. It served with the SOS until August 1919 when it returned to Camp Merritt, New Jersey. It was demobilized at Camp Gordon, Georgia in August 1919.

329th Service Battalion. The battalion was organized in May 1918 at Camp Grant, Illinois it moved to Camp Upton, New York in August 1918 and sailed for France from Hoboken, New Jersey. It served with the SOS until June 1919 when it returned to Camp Jackson, South Carolina. It was demobilized at Camp Shelby, Mississippi in July 1919.

330th Service Battalion. The battalion was organized in June 1918 at Camp Jackson, South Carolina it moved to Camp Wadsworth, South Carolina in June 1918. In August 1918 it moved to Camp Merritt, New Jersey and sailed for France from Hoboken, New Jersey in September 1918. It served with the SOS until September 1919 when it returned to Camp Merritt, New Jersey. It was demobilized at Camp Lee, Virginia in September 1919.

331st Service Battalion. The battalion was organized in May 1918 at Camp Travis, Texas it moved to Camp MacArthur, Texas and in July 1918 to Camp Hill, Virginia and sailed for France from Newport News, Virginia. It served with the SOS until July 1919 when it returned to Camp Jackson, South Carolina. It was demobilized at Camp Travis, Texas in July 1919.

332nd Service Battalion. The battalion was organized in July 1918 at Camp Travis, Texas it moved to Camp Hill, Virginia in July 1918 and sailed for France from Newport News, Virginia. It served with the SOS until July 1919 when it returned to Camp Mills, New York. It was demobilized at Camp Pike, Arkansas in July 1919.

333rd Service Battalion. The battalion was organized in July 1918 at Camp Meade, Maryland and sailed for France from Hoboken, New Jersey August 1918. It served with the SOS until June 1919 when it returned to Camp Upton, New York. It was demobilized at Camp Meade, Maryland in July 1919.

334th Service Battalion. The battalion was organized in May 1918 at Camp Shelby, Mississippi it moved to Camp Hill, Virginia in July 1918 and sailed for France from Newport News, Virginia. It served with the SOS until July 1919 when it returned to Camp Mills, New York. It was demobilized at Camp Pike, Arkansas in July 1919.

Opposite: This corporal from Headquarters, 343rd Labor Battalion sat for his picture when he returned home. Courtesy Private Collection.

Below: Unidentified black laborers dig graves somewhere in France. Courtesy National Archives.

Above: Cutting wood and lumber for use of the American Expeditionary Forces. 342nd Labor Battalion working the saw. Jonehary, Haute Marne, France. January 4, 1919. Courtesy National Archives.

Left: In this French Carte Postale, two friends stand by their barracks; the soldier on the right wears Quartermaster collar insignia. Courtesy Private Collection.

Opposite
Left: This unidentified soldier is wearing Quartermaster Corps insignia on his collar in this photo taken in France. Courtesy Private Collection.

Top right: A portrait of a soldier taken in Brest, France; this soldier is wearing an Advance Section Service of Supply insignia on his shoulder and an Infantry collar disk with HQ signifying Headquarters Company. Courtesy Private Collection.

Bottom right: Another soldier portrait from Brest, France; note the Advance Section Services of Supply shoulder sleeve insignia. Courtesy Private Collection.

An unidentified soldier toils to repair tracks in France. Courtesy Private Collection.

Opposite: Two soldiers pose together in a studio in Nantes, France. Courtesy Private Collection.

General Pershing reviewing 14,000 troops at Brest, France. These are the troops of the Advanced Section, Services of Supply and included many black soldiers. Courtesy Private Collection.

335th Service Battalion. The battalion was organized in June 1918 at Camp Pike, Arkansas it moved to Camp Stuart, Virginia in July 1918 and sailed for France from Newport News, Virginia. It served with the SOS until July 1919 when it returned to Camp Jackson, South Carolina. It was demobilized at Camp Shelby, Mississippi in July 1919.

336th Service Battalion. The battalion was organized in May 1918 in Camp Hill, Virginia and sailed for France from Newport News, Virginia in June 1918. It was absorbed by the 301st Stevedore Battalion August 1918.

337th Service Battalion. The battalion was organized in May 1918 in Camp Hill, Virginia and sailed for France from Newport News, Virginia in June 1918. It was absorbed by the 301st Stevedore Battalion July 1918.

338th Service Battalion. The battalion was organized in August 1918 at Camp Lee, Virginia it moved to Camp Hill, Virginia in August 1918 and sailed for France from Newport News, Virginia. It served with the SOS until July 1919 when it returned to Camp Mills, New York. It was demobilized at Camp Dix, New Jersey in July 1919.

339th Service Battalion. The battalion was organized in August 1918 at Camp Alexander, Virginia it moved to Camp Stuart, Virginia in August 1918 and sailed for France from Newport News, Virginia in September 1918. It served with the SOS until August 1919 when it returned to Camp Merritt, New Jersey. It was demobilized at Camp Lee, Virginia in August 1919.

340th Service Battalion. The battalion was organized in August 1918 at Camp Alexander, Virginia and sailed for France from Newport News, Virginia in September 1918. It served with the SOS until July 1919 when it returned to Camp Alexander, Virginia. It was demobilized at Camp Shelby, Mississippi in July 1919.

341st Service Battalion. The battalion was organized in August 1918 at Camp Alexander, Virginia and sailed for France from Newport News, Virginia in September 1918. It served with the SOS until July 1919 when it returned to Camp Mills, New York and was demobilized.

342nd Service Battalion. The battalion was organized in September 1918 at Camp Alexander, Virginia and sailed for France from Newport News, Virginia. It served with the SOS until July 1919 when it returned to Norfolk, Virginia. It was demobilized at Camp Gordon, Georgia in July 1919.

343rd Service Battalion. The battalion was organized in September 1918 at Camp Alexander, Virginia and sailed for France from Newport News, Virginia in October 1918. It served with the SOS until July 1919 when it returned to Camp Hill, Virginia and was demobilized.

344th Service Battalion. The battalion was organized in September 1918 at Camp Greene, North Carolina that month it moved to Camp Upton, New York and sailed

Gen Pershing reviewing 14,000. Troops at Brest. France

Three friends strike a pose. (From right to left) Louis Jones, New Orleans, Louisiana (note the Advanced Section Services of Supply shoulder sleeve insignia), Thomas Lytle also of New Orleans and a man simply noted as "Davis." Courtesy Private Collection.

Opposite
Bottom left: This cherished and badly worn image of an Advanced Section, Services of Supply soldier has the touching notation on the reverse, "My Arthur Cooper." Courtesy Private Collection.

Top right: In this first of four pictures from an unidentified soldier's photo album, a soldier poses on a horse in France. Courtesy Private Collection.

Botom right: An unknown soldier poses with a cigar somewhere in France. This photo is dated 1919. Courtesy Private Collection.

for France from Hoboken, New Jersey. It served with the SOS until June 1919 when it returned to Camp Lee, Virginia where it was demobilized.

345th Service Battalion. The battalion was organized in September 1918 at Camp Greene, North Carolina that month it moved to Camp Upton, New York and sailed for France from Hoboken, New Jersey. It served with the SOS until July 1919 when it returned to Camp Gordon, Georgia where it was demobilized.

346th Service Battalion. The battalion was organized in September 1918 at Camp Greene, North Carolina that month it moved to Camp Merritt, New Jersey and sailed for France from Hoboken, New Jersey. It served with the SOS until July 1919 when it returned to Camp Alexander, Virginia. It was demobilized at Camp Jackson, South Carolina that same month.

347th Service Battalion. The battalion was organized in September 1918 at Camp Greene, North Carolina. In October 1918 it moved to Camp Stuart, Virginia and sailed for France from Newport News, Virginia. It served with the SOS until June 1919 when it returned to Camp Alexander, Virginia. It was demobilized at Camp Lee, Virginia in July 1919.

348th Service Battalion. The battalion was organized in September 1918 at Camp Greene, North Carolina it moved to Camp Mills, New York in October 1918 and sailed for France from Hoboken, New Jersey. It served with the SOS until August 1919 when it returned to Camp Mills, New York. It was demobilized at Camp Lee, Virginia that same month.

349th Service Battalion. The battalion was organized in September 1918 at Camp Greene, North Carolina. In November 1918, it moved to Charleston, South Carolina it was demobilized there in April 1919.

Laundry and Service[22]
316th Mobile Laundry Company. Active in France with the SOS from July 1918 until August 1919. A Mobile Laundry Company had an aggregate strength of thirty-seven men. There were no officers assigned.[23]

Stevedore Regiments
A Stevedore Regiment had an aggregate strength of 2,498. It consisted of a regimental headquarters, headquarters and supply company, two battalions, and a medical department. Each battalion consisted of four companies; each company consisted of 253 soldiers (three officers and 250 enlisted men).[24]

301st Stevedore Regiment. The regiment was activated at Camp Hill, Virginia in September 1917 and sailed to France from Hoboken, New Jersey in October 1917. The unit was transferred to the Transportation Corps in September 1918. The 301st was active at the port of St. Nazaire.

302nd Stevedore Regiment. The regiment was activated at Camp Hill, Virginia in October 1917 and sailed to France from Hoboken, New Jersey in December 1917. The unit was transferred to the Transportation Corps in September 1918. The 301st was active at the port of Bordeaux.

303rd Stevedore Regiment. The regiment was activated at Camp Hill, Virginia in October 1917 and sailed to France from Hoboken, New Jersey in December 1917. The unit was transferred to the Transportation Corps in September 1918.

A bandsman strikes a pose with his instrument, France 1919. Courtesy Private Collection.

An interesting portrait of a musician corporal; note the musician's lyre below his stripes and on his overseas cap. He is also wearing an unidentified and unusual shoulder sleeve insignia. Courtesy Private Collection.

Left: This Brest, France portrait is of another musician; note the Private First Class Musicians insignia on his right sleeve. Courtesy Private Collection.

This the basic First Army insignia; the embroidered letter "A" designates the First Army all executed upon an olive drab background.

An unusual example of the First Army Pioneer Infantry insignia; this specimen uses the red letter "P" between the legs of the "A" to indicate pioneer infantry.

Armies

The American Expeditionary Forces ultimately created three Armies during the course of the war. Armies were generally composed of multiple corps and divisions along with necessary logistical support units for specific operations. While First and Second Army were "Fighting Units"; Third Army was created specifically for the Occupation. Many black units found themselves attached to Armies or Corps assigned principally in logistics roles.

First Army

Organized August 10, 1918 in the Regular Army at Le Ferte-sous-Jouarre, France and demobilized at Marseille April 20, 1919.[25]

Insignia
The black letter "A" signifies Army and alludes to the first letter of the alphabet, hence First Army. This insignia was approved in November of 1918. The First Army insignia often incorporates branch within the legs of the letter "A." Almost immediately the Corps Headquarters began the first of several attempts to inculcate basic designs to distinguish various subordinate elements of the corps. Primarily these designs were geometric patterns in red and white or in the basic branch color of the organization. These efforts culminated with Memorandum 45, dated 14 December 1918, which formally established a system for each major assigned branch. Despite this proactive measure, literally scores of variations of First Army patches are extant that do not follow the guidelines set forth in Memorandum 45. Oddly enough, varieties outside of regulation are far more common than those following the instructions of the memorandum.[26] A final variation of the insignia exists for the personnel working at First Army Headquarters. This insignia appears in two forms both of which incorporate a monogram of a red "A" and "R" to the left and right of a gold or yellow letter "H" upon which is superimposed a white number "1." This monogram is representative of headquarters First Army. One form appears on a dark blue circular background with a second form superimposed upon a red-bordered diamond. Doubtless, more varieties of the World War I First Army Patch exist than of any other army, corps or division insignia. Keller & Keller's publication, *United States Army Shoulder Patches and Related Insignia from World War I to Korea, Army Groups, Armies and Corps*, provides the best catalog of these variations.

Campaigns:
St. Mihiel operation, Meuse-Argonne, Lorraine 1918.

Commanding Generals:
General John J. Pershing, Lieutenant General Hunter Liggett.

Second Army

Second Army was organized September 20, 1918 at Toul, Meurthe-et-Moselle. The unit was demobilized April 15, 1919 in France.[27]

Insignia
On a green background the numeral "2" with the top red and the bottom white suggesting the unit designation and the red and white representative of the colors found on the army standard. The insignia was approved on December 11, 1918. An alternate version exists bearing a block figure "B". This design was originally prepared based on the idea that if First Army was an "A" Second should wear a "B". This style was never officially sanctioned.

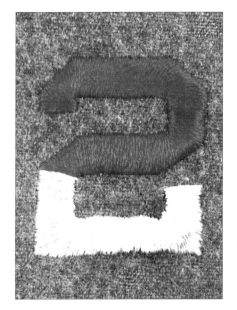

Far left: A fully embroidered Second Army insignia.

Left: This fully embroidered Second Army insignia uses the "B" coupled with an inset 4th Corps insignia to designate the wearer as Second Army, 4th Corps.

Campaigns:
Lorraine 1918[28]

Commanding Generals:
General John J. Pershing, Lieutenant General Robert L. Bullard.

Third Army

The Third Army was organized at Ligny-en-Barrois, France between 7 and 15 November 1918 and was demobilized on July 2, 1919 in Germany.[29]

Insignia

The insignia consisted of a blue disc with a white letter "A" within a red circle forming the monogram "A O O" emblematic of Army of Occupation, the principal duty of the Army following the 1918 Armistice. The disc with two borders alludes to the numerical designation (3) of the unit. There is a variant insignia with the letter "C" following the "A" as First Army, "B" as Second Army and "C" as Third Army. This insignia was never authorized.

Campaigns:
None.

Commanding Generals:
Major General Joseph T. Dickman, Major General Edward F. McGlachlin, Jr., Lieutenant General Hunter Liggett.

Colored Army Troops

Engineers[30]
The Historical Report of the Chief Engineer American Expeditionary Forces lists the assignment of Engineer Regiments as follows[31]:

First Army Area: 527th, 537th, 544th, 545th, 546th, 603rd
Second Army Area: 505th, 508th, 524th, 530th

The Third Army insignia.

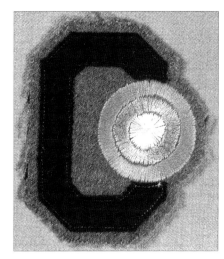

The "C" pattern Third Army insignia with roundel indicating Third Army Air Service.

505th Engineer Service Battalion. The battalion was organized in October 1917 at Camp Lee, Virginia and sailed for France from Newport News, Virginia in December 1917. The unit served with Army troops until May 1919 when it returned to Camp Merritt, New Jersey and was demobilized the same month at Camp Meade, Maryland.

508th Engineer Service Battalion. The battalion was organized in October 1917 at Camp Pike, Arkansas and sailed for France from Hoboken, New Jersey in January 1918. The unit served with Army troops until June 1919 when it returned to Camp Alexander, Virginia and was demobilized the same month at Camp Shelby, Mississippi.

513th Engineer Service Battalion. The battalion was organized in January 1918 at Camp Travis, Texas, it was transferred to Camp Stuart, Virginia in March 1918 and sailed for France from Newport News, Virginia in April 1918. The unit served with Army troops until June 1919 when it returned to Camp Upton, New York and was demobilized the same month at Camp Bowie, Texas.

516th Engineer Service Battalion. The battalion was organized in April 1918 at Camp Gordon, Georgia; it was transferred to Camp A.A. Humphreys, Virginia in June 1918 and sailed for France from Hoboken, New Jersey in July 1918. The unit served with Army troops until July 1919 when it returned to Camp Alexander, Virginia and was demobilized the same month at Camp Gordon, Georgia.

522nd Engineer Service Battalion. The battalion was organized in March 1918 at Camp Meade, Maryland; it was assigned to Camp A.A. Humphreys, Virginia in April. It sailed for France from Hoboken, New Jersey in August 1918. The unit served with Army troops until June 1919 when it returned to Camp Alexander, Virginia. It was demobilized at Camp Bowie, Texas in the same month.

524th Engineer Service Battalion. The battalion was organized in April 1918 at Camp Pike, Arkansas it was transferred to Camp A.A. Humphreys, Virginia in May 1918 and then to Camp Stuart, Virginia in June 1918. The battalion sailed for France from Newport News, Virginia in July 1918. It served with Army troops until June 1919 when it returned to Camp Jackson, South Carolina and was demobilized.

527th Engineer Service Battalion. The battalion was organized in March 1918 at Camp Dodge, Iowa; it was transferred to Camp Upton, New York in April 1918 and sailed for France from Hoboken, New Jersey in June 1918. The unit served with Army troops until July 1919 when it returned to Camp Upton, New York and was demobilized the same month at Camp Gordon, Georgia.

528th Engineer Service Battalion. The battalion was organized in April 1918 at Camp Dodge, Iowa and sailed for France from Hoboken, New Jersey in July 1918. The unit served with Army troops until June 1919 when it returned to Camp Upton, New York and was demobilized the same month at Camp Gordon, Georgia.

529th Engineer Service Battalion. The battalion was organized in April 1918 at Camp Funston, Kansas and sailed for France from Hoboken, New Jersey in June 1918. The unit served with Army troops until June 1919 when it returned to Camp Upton, New York and was demobilized.

530th Engineer Service Battalion. The battalion was organized in April 1918 at Camp Funston, Kansas and sailed for France from Hoboken, New Jersey in July 1918. The unit served with Army troops until June 1919 when it returned to Camp Upton, New York and was demobilized.

532nd Engineer Service Battalion. The battalion was organized in May 1918 at Camp Zachary Taylor, Kentucky it was transferred to Camp Stuart, Virginia in July 1918 and sailed for France from Newport News, Virginia in the same month. The unit served with Army troops until July 1919 when it returned to Camp Mills, New York and was demobilized later in the month at Camp Zachary Taylor, Kentucky

534th Engineer Service Battalion. The battalion was organized in May 1918 at Camp Jackson, South Carolina and assigned to Camp Upton, New York in August 1918. It sailed for France from Hoboken, New Jersey the sane month. The unit served with Army troops until July 1919 when it returned to Camp Devens, Massachusetts and was demobilized.

535th Engineer Service Battalion. The battalion was organized in May 1918 at Camp Lee, Virginia. It sailed for France from Newport News, Virginia in August 1918. The unit served with Army troops until July 1919 when it returned to Camp Upton, New York and was demobilized.

537th Engineer Battalion. The battalion was organized in May 1918 at Camp Travis, Texas. In July, It was transferred to Camp Mills, New York and sailed for France from Hoboken, New Jersey later that month. The unit served with Army troops until July 1919 when it returned to Camp Devens, Massachusetts and was demobilized at Camp Bowie, Texas.

539th Engineer Service Battalion. The battalion was organized in May 1918 at Camp Gordon, Georgia. In September it sailed for France from Hoboken, New Jersey. The unit served with Army troops until June 1919 when it returned to Camp Upton, New York and was demobilized in July at Camp Gordon, Georgia.

541st Engineer Service Battalion. The battalion was organized in August 1918 at Camp Humphreys, Virginia. It sailed for France from Hoboken, New Jersey in September 1918. The unit served with Army troops until July 1919 when it returned to Camp Upton, New York and was demobilized Camp Dix, New Jersey.

542nd Engineer Service Battalion. The battalion was organized in August 1918 at Camp Humphreys, Virginia. It sailed for France from Hoboken, New Jersey in September 1918. The unit served with Army troops until June 1919 when it returned to Camp Upton, New York and was demobilized Camp Dix, New Jersey.

543rd Engineer Service Battalion. The battalion was organized in August 1918 at Camp Humphreys, Virginia. It sailed for France from Hoboken, New Jersey in September 1918. The unit served with Army troops until June 1919 when it returned to Camp Alexander, Virginia. The battalion was demobilized Camp Lee, Virginia in July.

544th Engineer Service Battalion. The battalion was organized in August 1918 at Camp Humphreys, Virginia. It sailed for France from Hoboken, New Jersey in September 1918. The unit served with Army troops until July 1919 when it returned to, Norfolk, Virginia. The battalion was demobilized Camp Lee, Virginia in July.

546th Engineer Service Battalion. The battalion was organized in September 1918 at Camp Humphreys, Virginia. It sailed for France from Hoboken, New Jersey in September 1918. The unit served with Army troops until June 1919 when it returned to, Newport News, Virginia. The battalion was demobilized Camp Jackson, South Carolina later that month.

Pioneer Infantry[32]

The Historical Report of the Chief Engineer American Expeditionary Forces lists the assignment of Pioneer Regiments as follows[33]:

First Army Area: 805th, 807th, 815th
Second Army Area: 803rd, 804th, 806th, 813th

803rd Pioneer Infantry Regiment. The regiment was organized at Camp Grant, Illinois in July 1918 it moved to Camp Upton, New York in September and then sailed to France that month from Hoboken, New Jersey. It served on railroad construction duty with Second Army Engineers until July 1919 when it returned to Newport News, Virginia and was demobilized at Camp Grant, Illinois that same month. The unit was commanded by Colonel M.L. McGraw.

804th Pioneer Infantry Regiment. The regiment was organized at Camp Dodge, Iowa in July 1918 it moved to Camp Upton, New York in August and then sailed to France in September from Hoboken, New Jersey. It served with Second Army until July 1919 when it returned to Camp Mills, New York and was demobilized at Camp Gordon, Georgia that same month. The unit was commanded by Colonel S.P. Lyon

Corporal A. Hayes, Company L, 807th Pioneer Infantry Regiment. Note that Hayes is armed with a pistol and holds a small binocular case in his left hand. Courtesy Private Collection.

Private Robert Stevens, Company H, 803rd Pioneer Infantry Regiment in France. Courtesy Military History Institute.

805th Pioneer Infantry Regiment[34] "The Bearcats". The regiment was organized at Camp Funston, Kansas in June 1918 it moved to Camp Upton, New York in August and then sailed to France in September from Quebec, Canada. The Regiment included twenty-five men from the seasoned 25th Infantry Regiment, and in January 1918, Colonel C.B. Humphrey issued a letter commending the "conscientious and intelligent work" of the officers and men of the 805th. These accolades were echoed by the First Army Chief Engineer, Colonel George R. Spalding.[35] It built roads and light railways under the Second Army Engineers until July 1919 when it returned to Camp Upton, New York and was demobilized at Camp Shelby, Mississippi in July. The unit was commanded by Colonel Chauncey B. Humphrey.

806th Pioneer Infantry Regiment. The regiment was organized at Camp Funston, Kansas in July 1918 in September, it moved to Camp Mills, New York and sailed to France later in the month from Hoboken, New Jersey. The 806th boasted a peculiar reputation. It is said that an order was published that mandated "only handsome men for the 806th." Mention of their good looks was heard wherever they traveled in France. This reputation by no means hampered their work ethic and diligence. In fact, the 806th helped to construct the celebrated Pershing Stadium in Paris.[36] It also built roads under the First and Second Army Engineers until June 1919 when it

Corporal Frank Saunders of the 315th Pioneer Infantry Regiment putting a little American "Pep" into a Frenchman's drum. Glorieux, Meuse, France. January 4, 1919. Courtesy National Archives.

returned to Camp Upton, New York and was demobilized at Camp Shelby, Mississippi in July. The unit was commanded by Colonel C. Williams.

807th Pioneer Infantry Regiment. The regiment was organized at Camp Dix, New Jersey in July 1918 in September; it sailed to France from Hoboken, New Jersey. By command of General Pershing, the Regiment was awarded the Silver Band to be engraved and placed upon the Pike of Colors of Lance of the Standard for its' participation in the Meuse-Argonne Offensive, October 25th to November 11th 1918.[37] It also performed construction work under the First Army Engineers until July 1919 when it returned to Newport News, Virginia and was demobilized at Camp Jackson, South Carolina.

808th Pioneer Infantry Regiment. The regiment was organized at Camp Meade, Maryland in July 1918 in August; it sailed to France from Hoboken, New Jersey. The 808th was the first of these Regiments to arrive in France, landing at Brest on September 7th, 1918.[38] It performed salvage work, road and narrow gauge railroad construction under the First and Second Army Engineers until June 1919 when it returned to Camp Alexander, Virginia and was demobilized at Camp Lee, Virginia. The unit was commanded by Colonel H. Kinnison.

809th Pioneer Infantry Regiment. The regiment was organized at Camp Dodge, Iowa in August 1918; the unit moved to Camp Upton, New York in September and it sailed to France from Hoboken, New Jersey. This Regiment is accredited with a larger percentage of professional and skilled artisans than most of the others. These included such notables as Howard Drew; the hundred yard dash world-champion, and Messers Dismukes, Lyons, Malacher and Charleston of baseball fame.[39] It performed labor under Army Engineers until July 1919 when it returned to Camp Mills, New York and was demobilized at Camp Sherman, Ohio. The unit was commanded by Colonel W.S. Mapes.

811th Pioneer Infantry Regiment. The regiment was organized at Camp Dix, New Jersey in August 1918; the unit sailed to France from Hoboken, New Jersey in October 1918. It performed stevedore work until July 1919 when it returned to Camp Mills, New York and was demobilized at Camp Dix, New Jersey. The unit was commanded by Colonel D.G. Davids.

813th Pioneer Infantry Regiment. The regiment was organized at Camp Sherman, Ohio in August 1918; the unit moved to Camp Mills, New York and sailed to France from Hoboken, New Jersey in September 1918. Under the leadership of Sergeant Major Williams of the famed 24th Infantry, the Regiment possessed a fighting spirit. One its' men reflected this spirit in the following declaration: "We endured all hardships of the front but missed the thing we wanted most-some real whacks at the enemy."[40] It performed road, salvage, and mortuary affairs as Army troops until July 1919 when it returned to Camp Alexander, Virginia and was demobilized at Camp Dix, New Jersey. The unit was commanded by Colonel J.E. Morris.

815th Pioneer Infantry Regiment. The regiment was organized at Camp Funston, Kansas in September 1918; the unit moved to Camp Merritt, New Jersey and sailed to France from Hoboken, New Jersey in September 1918. It performed road work with First Army Engineers until July 1919 when it returned to Camp Stuart, Virginia and was demobilized at Camp Travis, Texas. The unit was commanded by Colonel L.P. Butler.

816th Pioneer Infantry Regiment. The regiment was organized at Camp Funston, Kansas in September 1918; the unit moved to Camp Upton, New York and sailed to France from Hoboken, New Jersey in October 1918. It performed work with First Army Engineers until August 1919 when it returned to Camp Alexander, Virginia and was demobilized at Camp Shelby, Mississippi. The unit was commanded by Colonel L.A. Chapman.

*Corporal Sampson G. Morse of Company G, 808th Pioneer Infantry Regiment, taking a nap on a pile of shells.
Between Esnes and Montzeville, Meuse, France. October 12, 1918. Courtesy National Archives.*

*View of winning team. Colored team, 809th Pioneer Infantry Regiment, Nantes Champions White League Base
Section Number 1 verses Colored Champion League Base Section Number 1 at Savenay, Loire Inferieure, France,
May 23, 1919. Courtesy National Archives.*

Baptismal service; 811th Pioneer Infantry Companies I & K, 312th Labor Battalion. Services conducted by Chaplin Edward C. Kimble, U.S. Army (preaching) and Arrington C. Hall, Colored YMCA Secretary. The two candidates for baptism can be seen sitting on a bench in front row. Mr. Hall, YMCA Secretary on front bench , candidates on right. The darkest is Private Albert Stevens; the lighter one is Lenzie Saunders. Lieutenant Colonel Rice can be seen to the right of the candidates. Captain Briggs, Commander of Company I is in service cap behind the candidates. Rochefort-sur-Mer, Charente Inferieure, France. January 26, 1919. Courtesy National Archives.

Members of Company B, 803rd Pioneer Infantry digging entrenchments. Between Cheppy and Varennes-en-Argonne, Meuse, France. October 1918. Courtesy National Archives.

Two unidentified Pioneer Infantry soldiers pose with P-17 Enfield rifles in France. The soldier on the right wears the rank of a Private First Class. Courtesy Private Collection.

An unidentified soldier stands in front of his barracks building holding a P-17 Enfield and wearing a driver's cap. Courtesy Private Collection.

An unknown infantry private poses in France; he wears infantry branch insignia with an F Company letter on his overseas cap. Courtesy Private Collection.

Left: A Pioneer Infantryman stands resolutely with his P-17 Rifle. Courtesy Private Collection.

Below: An unidentified infantry soldier from Company C of an unknown Pioneer Regiment poses in a French studio. Courtesy Private Collection.

Opposite: Two men possibly pioneer infantrymen stand with Model P-17 rifles and rubber trench boots in France. Courtesy Private Collection.

The 803rd Pioneer Infantry Band at Charnberry, France, March 18, 1919. Addy Hunton sits at the center of the formation. Courtesy Private Collection.

Salvation Army workers giving fresh donuts to the soldiers just in from the lines. Varennes-en-Argonne, Meuse, France. October 12, 1918. Courtesy National Archives.

Infantryman Riley Goldsmith poses in a French studio. Courtesy Private Collection.

A young infantryman stands in a French farmyard with his Model 1917 U.S. Enfield rifle. Courtesy Private Collection.

Two soldiers in France with Model 1917 U.S. Enfield rifles. Courtesy Private Collection.

An unidentified infantryman stands in front of a French farmhouse carrying his pistol and ready for a fight. Courtesy Private Collection.

This unidentified Pioneer Infantryman wears his regiment's numbers on his overseas cap, unfortunately, only the first digit of the three digit number is visible. He holds the Model 1917 U.S. Enfield rifle. Courtesy Private Collection.

Two soldiers pose; both men wear F Company Infantry insignia; on the reverse of the photo is scrawled, "When I was in service." Courtesy Private Collection.

An infantry First Sergeant (far left) sits with two of his soldiers (wearing British tunics and American insignia).
Courtesy Private Collection.

Major General Eli L. Helmick decorating men with Distinguished Service Cross medals for exceptional bravery;
Brest, France. January 27, 1919. Courtesy National Archives.

Colored Soldiers in the Army Corps

Army Corps generally consisted of three to five divisions and supporting organizations tailored for combat operations. Before the war ended, the American Expeditionary Forces created nine corps.

Fully embroidered I Corps insignia.

I Corps

The First Corps was organized at Neufchateau, France 15-20 January 1918. It was demobilized in France on March 25, 1919.[41]

Insignia
The Corps chose a black disc with a white border. The disk was the insignia of the First Corps, during the Civil War and was one of the hardest fighting corps in the Army of the Potomac. Under the command of Major General John F. Reynolds, this corps was largely credited with saving the Federal Army on the first day of the battle of Gettysburg. This most certainly was a factor in the decision to retain the insignia.

Campaigns:
Champagne-Marne, Aisne-Marne, St. Michiel, Meuse-Argonne, Ile de France 1918, Champagne 1918. Lorraine 1918.[42]

II Corps

The corps was organized February 24, 1918 at Montreuil, France and demobilized February 1, 1919 at LeMans, France.[43]

Insignia
This corps incorporated the traditional colors of blue and white, which stem from the use of these colors on the standard of a field corps. The insignia consists of a blue rectangle, bordered white, with the Roman numeral II flanked by a rampant Lion (sinister) and rising Eagle (dexter) facing each other. The Lion and Eagle are representative of the combined nature of this corps. The II Corps was composed of troops from Britain and the United States; the Lion symbolizes Britain and the Eagle symbolizes the United States.

Campaigns:
Somme Offensive.[44]

This fully embroidered insignia of the II Corps features the Eagle representing the United States along with the Lion representing England. The II Corps was a combined U.S./UK Corps.

III Corps

Third Corps was organized May 16, 1918 at Mussy-sur-Seine, France and demobilized on August 9, 1919 at Camp Sherman, Ohio.[45]

Insignia
The insignia of the Third Corps incorporates the field corps blue and white color scheme. The insignia is in the shape of a caltrop: a defensive device which when dropped always lands with one of its pointed spikes pointing upward. This device was used against mounted and dismounted troops since antiquity. The profile shows three of the points in blue alluding to the corps number with a triangular center in white.

Campaigns:
Aisne-Marne, Oise-Aisne, Meuse-Argonne, Champagne 1918, Lorraine 1918.[46]

The III Corps chose the three-pointed caltrop as their insignia; this is the standard die cut variety.

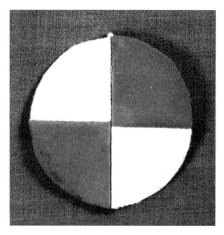

This is a standard example of a felt on felt IV Corps insignia.

This is the standard V Corps insignia; a fully embroidered pentagon in white filled with blue wedges.

This example of the VI Corps insignia is embroidered on felt.

IV Corps

The corps was organized June 20, 1918 at Neufchateau, France and demobilized on May 11, 1919.[47]

Insignia
The insignia of the IV Corps also incorporates the field corps blue and white color scheme. Their insignia is a disc divided into four equal parts of alternating blue and white fields alluding to the corps number

Campaigns:
St. Mihiel, Lorraine 1918.[48]

V Corps

The corps was organized between July 7-12, 1918 at Remiremont, France and was demobilized May 2, 1919 at Camp, Kansas.[49]

Insignia
The insignia of V Corps generally incorporates the blue and white colors of a field corps. The insignia is the five-sided blue pentagon bordered in white and divided into five wedges. Variations exist using different colored wedges to designate subordinate units within the corps. Some of the known examples of this practice include V Corps Artillery which replaced the bottom blue wedge of the pentagon with a red wedge, or replaced all the blue wedges with red wedges, V Corps Cavalry which replaced all the blue wedges with yellow wedges, V Corps Infantry which substitutes a light blue wedge for the bottom wedge, and V Corps Signal which replaces the white background with orange.

Campaigns:
St. Mihiel, Meuse-Argonne, Lorraine 1918.[50]

VI Corps

The Sixth Corps was organized between July 23 and August 1, 1918 at Neufchateau, France and demobilized at Camp Devens, Massachusetts in May 1919.[51]

Insignia
The VI Corps insignia is that of a blue disc with a white numeral "6" superimposed; representing the corps number.

Campaigns:
Lorraine 1918.[52]

VII Corps

The corps was formed at Remiremont, France on August 19, 1918 and demobilized at Camp Upton, New York from July 9-11, 1919.[53]

Insignia
The insignia of the VII Corps is a shield in blue with a white numeral 7 representative of the corps designation.

Campaigns:
Streamer with Inscription.[54]

VIII Corps

Eighth Corps was formed between November 26-29, 1918 at Montigny-sur-Aube (Cote-D'Or), France and was demobilized April 20, 1919 in France.[55]

Insignia
A blue octagon bordered in white alluding to the number of the corps, with the white numeral "8" superimposed which is also representative of the numerical designation.

Campaigns:
None.

IX Corps

The corps was formed November 25-29, 1918 at Ligny-en-Barrois, France and demobilized May 5, 1919 in France.[56]

Insignia
Ninth corps did not follow the blue and white color scheme normally used by corps level units. They chose a blue disk bordered in red with the red Roman Numeral IX representative of the corps numerical designation.

Campaigns:
None.

Corps Troops
814th Pioneer Infantry Regiment. The regiment was organized at Camp Zachary Taylor, Kentucky in August 1918; the unit moved to Camp Upton, New York and sailed to France from Hoboken, New Jersey in October 1918. It served with Corps troops until December 1918 when it returned to Camp Mills, New York and was demobilized at Camp Zachery Taylor, Kentucky. The unit was commanded by Colonel C.A. Dolph.

The standard VII Corps insignia design embroidered on felt.

This standard VIII Corps insignia is embroidered on wool felt.

The typical IX Corps insignia embroidered upon wool felt background.

The original Signal Corps caption reads: Sambo and his bouquet at Reuilly Barracks. Courtesy National Archives.

Opposite

Top: In an image reminiscent of Matthew Brady's iconic Gettysburg battlefield photograph, two black soldiers survey the damages at one of the first towns captured by Americans during the Battle of the Argonne. Malancourt, Meuse, France. November 10, 1918. Courtesy National Archives.

Bottom: A group of non-commissioned officers and men arrive in France and pose in the field with their officer rear row, far left. Courtesy Private Collection.

"Back Home" tells the story of this photograph. It is a close up of "Holy Smoke" who though wounded is still able to show his teeth. Courtesy National Archives.

Right: This soldier posed with a swagger stick topped with an '03 Springfield rifle cartridge. The reverse of the photo bears a Terre Haute, Indiana address. Courtesy Private Collection.

An unknown soldier stands in front of a building. Courtesy Private Collection.

Private Davis from Knoxville, Tennessee sent this photo home to his "Dirst (sic) sister" with the message that he was "somewhere in France." Courtesy Private Collection.

Two veterans of six months in France pose with weapons in front of their billets. Courtesy Private Collection.

Soldiers await call to mess in their barracks in France.
Courtesy Private Collection.

Left: Private Martin Gordon of Clinton, Indiana poses for a photograph in France. Courtesy Private Collection.

Opposite: Two unknown friends, who appear to be battle hardened veterans, pose together in France. Courtesy Private Collection.

Below: A young soldier stands outside his barracks in France; his name forgotten, his deeds never will be. Courtesy Private Collection.

Opposite: This Carte Postale from France was addressed to Robert Coleman in Washington, D.C.; these two friends appear ready to return home. Courtesy Private Collection.

Below: The first of two images of the same soldier shows an unknown soldier as a new recruit in training. Courtesy Private Collection.

Ready to return to the States, this striking image shows the same soldier as a veteran infantryman holding a bible. Courtesy Private Collection.

Left: A spectacular French portrait of an unknown soldier. Courtesy Private Collection.

Below: A loaded troopship arrives in New York; an unknown black regiment happy to be home. Note the group of white officers at center of photograph. Courtesy Private Collection.

Opposite: A poignant photo from France; all we know of this soldier is that it was sent to "Lile Harrell" in 1918 and doubtless cherished by her for years. Courtesy Private Collection.

Left: Fresh from the Front! This soldier holds his overcoat in this left arm and projects quite a martial image in this French studio portrait. Courtesy Private Collection.

Opposite
Left: H.C. Duke of Trinity, Texas poses in France. Courtesy Private Collection.

Right: The reverse of this French photo reads, "Dispatcher Troy Whitlock, Barracks Photo." Courtesy Private Collection.

Above: Two field soldiers stand together in France. Courtesy Private Collection.

Right: An unhappy looking soldier poses for the camera in a French studio. Courtesy Private Collection.

Opposite: Two soldiers stand in shirtsleeves in a French courtyard. Courtesy Private Collection.

Opposite
Top: An unknown unit poses with white officers at center. Courtesy Private Collection.

Middle: Soldiers watch a sporting contest in France. It appears that two men are about to run an obstacle course. Courtesy Private Collection.

Bottom: Unknown black soldiers load supplies onto Forty and Eight railway cars under supervision of white officers. Courtesy National Archives.

Right: This French studio portrait of a young soldier uses French and American flags as a backdrop for dramatic effect. Courtesy Private Collection.

Below: In this unusual photo, a First Army soldier wears an unidentified patch below his overseas stripe in the shape of a French Poodle. Courtesy Private Collection.

CHAPTER TWO

THE AMERICAN EXPEDITIONARY FORCES:
COMBAT DIVISIONS AND COLORED REGIMENTS

First Lieutenant Robert L. Campbell, Company I, 368th Infantry shown here just after his discharge from the hospital for wounds suffered in the Argonne. He was the first member of the 92nd Division to receive the Distinguished Service Cross. Courtesy National Archives.

92nd Infantry Division (Colored)

The War Department established the division on October 24, 1917 at Camps Grant, Upton, Dix, Meade, Dodge, Sherman, and Funston. The division was to be made up of black American selected service men from all parts of the United States. Headquarters, 183rd Infantry Brigade, 165th Infantry Regiment and the 350th Machine Gun Battalion mustered at Camp Grant, Headquarters, 184th Infantry Brigade, 167th Infantry Regiment and the 351st Machine Gun Battalion mustered at Camp Upton, Headquarters, 167th Field Artillery Brigade, 349th and 350th Field Artillery mustered at Camp Dix, the 368th Infantry and 351st Filed Artillery mustered at Camp Meade, the 366th Infantry mustered at Camp Dodge, the 317th Engineer Regiment and 325th Field Signal Battalion mustered at Camp Sherman, and the Division Headquarters, 349th Machine Gun Battalion, and trains mustered at Camp Funston.[1] The division was popularly known as the "Buffalo Division" calling upon the deeds of the famous Buffalo Soldiers of the Western Campaigns (black American troops were dubbed Buffalo Soldiers by Native Americans).

Insignia

The division insignia was a black buffalo on an olive drab disc bordered black. Approved December 6, 1918. Variants of the insignia exist with blue and red backgrounds, red purportedly representing the division artillery.[2] A separate insignia exists for the 349th Field Artillery which consists of a red swastika upon a diamond background with a white dot superimposed.[3] The adoption of the swastika for the 349th Field Artillery resulted from the white artillery officers of the regiment refusing to wear the Buffalo patch which was so closely linked to black soldiers; as such they considered the wear of the Buffalo Patch demeaning.

Campaigns:

Meuse-Argonne Offensive, Marbache.[4]

Division Organization (1917-1919):[5]

183rd Infantry Brigade:

365th Infantry Regiment
366th Infantry Regiment
350th Machine Gun Battalion

The standard insignia for the 92nd Division features felt on felt construction with stitching used to highlight the Buffalo.

An embroidered on felt version of the 92nd Division insignia.

In this example, the Buffalo faces right; felt on felt with stitching used to highlight the design.

184th Infantry Brigade:
367th Infantry Regiment
368th Infantry Regiment
351st Machine Gun Battalion

Division Troops:
349th Machine Gun Battalion

167th Field Artillery Brigade:
349th Field Artillery Regiment
350th Field Artillery Regiment
351st Field Artillery Regiment
317th Trench Mortar Battery

Division Support:
317th Engineer Regiment
325th Field Signal Battalion
317th Train Headquarters and Military Police
317th Ammunition Train
317th Supply Train
317th Engineer Train
317th Sanitary Train (35th, 366th, 367th, 368th Ambulance Companies & Field Hospitals)

A blue embroidered buffalo on French Horizon Blue material suggests French manufacture and possible use by 92nd Division Artillery personnel.

Division Combat Narrative:[6]
The first unit of the division arrived in France June 19, 1918; the last element July 18, 1918.

For training purposes, the division (less artillery) was sent to the 11th Training Area, with headquarters at Bourbonne-les-Bains (Haute-Marne). For the same purpose, the artillery brigade went to La Courtine (Creuse). It rejoined the division in the Marbache Sector (Lorraine) Oct. 21, 1918. On August 11, the division went to the Vosges with headquarters at Bruyères. On August 24, it commenced the relief of the 5th Division in the St. Dié Sector, completing the relief August 31. It remained in line until September 21, when it proceeded to the vicinity of Triaucourt (Meuse).

On September 25 the division, less the 368th Infantry and the artillery brigade constituted the reserve of the First Army Corps in the Meuse-Argonne Offensive, and was assembled in the woods northwest of Clermont. The 368th Infantry formed a part of the combat liaison between the French 4th Army and the American First Army September 26 to October 4, 1918. On September 29th the division, less one infantry brigade, the artillery and the engineers, was placed at the disposal

A fine example of a Liberty Loan type 92nd Division insignia.

Right: Embroidered version of a 92nd Division Artillery insignia.

Far right: Felt on felt construction is used for this 92nd Division Artillery insignia.

Opposite: C. Clarke, bugler , 15th New York Infantry [369th Regiment], Champagne 1918 by Raymond Desvarreaux, Courtesy West Point Museum Art Collection, U.S. Military Academy

Barbering in 317th Supply Train, 92nd Division. Belleville, Meuse, France. October 12, 1918. Courtesy National Archives.

of the 38th French Army Corps operating in the Argonne Forest where it formed the reserve of the French 1st Dismounted Cavalry Division. On October 3 it was relieved and placed at the disposal of the First American Army, and assigned as 1st Corps Reserve. On October 4 it was assigned to the Fourth American Corps and proceeded to the vicinity of Toul where on October 9 it relieved the 69th French Division in the Marbache Sector. It passed from the Fourth Corps to the Sixth Corps on October 25. The division participated in the attack of the Second American Army November 10-11, 1918, operating west of the Seille River along the heights on both banks of the Moselle River in the direction of Corny.

Days in the Front Line: 7 (training) 56 (sector) 0 (battle) for a total of 63. During operations the division took 38 prisoners and its casualties totaled 182 soldiers killed in action or died of wounds, 1,465 wounded in action.[7]

After the armistice the division remained in the occupied area until the middle of December when it proceeded to the Le Mans Embarkation Center preparatory to its return to the United States.[8]

Division Headquarters sailed from Brest on February 7, 1919, and arrived at New York on February 17, 1919.

The division had three commanding generals; Major General Charles C. Ballou, Major General Charles H. Martin, and Brigadier General James B. Erwin.

The gallant "Buffalo Division" received several citations and awards for courageous and distinguished conduct on the battlefields of France. In all, the Distinguished Service Cross was awarded to fourteen black officers and forty-three enlisted men for conspicuous bravery in action. There were also many other commendations to individuals and entire units such as the 367th Regiment.

The 367th Infantry Regiment is often noted with particular reference as it is considered to be the most successful regiment of the Buffalo Division.

As an example, in a 1919 edition of the Army Navy Journal the following excerpt attests to their combat performance. "Colored troops forming the 92nd Division of the A.E.F. have recently been awarded many honors. The entire 1st Battalion of the 367th Infantry have been cited for bravery and awarded the Croix de Guerre by the French military authorities. The citation was made because of the bravery and fine service of the battalion in the last engagement of the war, the drive toward Metz on November 10 and 11."[9]

The regiment's splendid record is greatly attributable to it's' commander, Colonel James A. Moss, and the relationship between him and the officers and men of the 367th. It is significant, in the social setting of 1917-1918, that a white officer of southern heritage was able to transcend that particular breeding and learn to appreciate the true value and capabilities black soldiers. Colonel Moss determined to treat the black officers and men entrusted to his leadership as American soldiers, and accord them a full measure of respect, opportunity and credit. In his words; "If properly trained and instructed, the colored man makes as good a soldier as the world as ever seen. The history of the Negro in all our wars … shows this … Make the colored man feel that you have faith in him, and then, by sympathetic and conscientious

training and instruction, help him to fit himself in a military way to vindicate that faith … Be strict with him, but treat him fairly and justly, making him realize that in your dealings with him he will always be given a square deal … In other words, treat and handle the colored man as you would any other human being out of whom you make a good soldier, out of whom you would get the best there is in him, and you will have as good a soldier as history has ever known."[10]

The success of the 367th Infantry Regiment brought out in bold relief two facts that, if fairly evaluated and applied, discounted the doubts and mindset challenging the capabilities of black combat soldiers and units pervasive during the early twentieth century. First, whenever, white men are placed in command of black troops, they should be of high intellectual and moral caliber, and secondly, black officers possess the intellectual acumen, and moral courage to command troops – at that time, of their own race – but as the veil of racial discrimination diminished, all American troops of any racial, ethnic or cultural composition.

As noted in the introduction, much suspicion existed regarding the capability of black men to effectively learn and discharge the duties of an artillerist. At the highest levels in the War Department, it was often questioned whether or not an artillery brigade composed of black soldiers could be sufficiently trained in the techniques of artillery to produce an effective unit. The tactics, techniques and procedures demanded by this branch required men of sufficient education and intellect to manipulate fractions, read scales, deflections, and accurately interpret other technical details. The draft did not produce in sufficient numbers, enough black men to form the artillery regiments. So the War Department broke with its' initial reluctance to recruit and accept black volunteer enlistments and instituted a special canvass to identify and recruit a sufficient number of qualified men to make up the 167th Field Artillery Brigade. Tuskegee Institute answered the call with a group of students, as did the cities of Baltimore, Pittsburg, and others. Groups of qualified men from high schools, churches and other organizations provided the great bulk enlistments.

As a result of this special canvass, the 167th Field Artillery Brigade, consisting of three regiments comprised the first black artillery brigade ever organized in the

Above: 368th Infantry Regiment, advancing to the front on camouflaged roads. Binarville, Marne, France. October 1, 1918. Courtesy National Archives.

Opposite
Top left: The three Negroes in the foreground digging a hole are from the 317th Engineers, 1st Army. Left to right: Corporal John Walker; Private Ben Williams, and Private Wade Dawkins. The Bosche apparently did nothing to repair the roads in three years and as a result they quickly break down under heavy traffic. 317th Engineers, one mile north of Varennes, on the way to Montblainville, Meuse, France. October 25, 1918. Courtesy National Archives.

Top right: View of Blacksmith Shop, 365th Infantry Regiment; Sergieux, Meuse, France, August 11, 1918. Courtesy National Archives.

Bottom: "Big Nims" with gas mask, 366th Infantry, 3rd Battalion Ainvelle, Vosges, France. August 8, 1918. This copy was annotated, "Happy Something struck this American Negro soldier as funny and he paused to laugh even during the gas mask drill." Courtesy Military History Institute.

world. During the training period and afterward on the battlefield, General John H. Sherburne frequently expressed the opinion that his artillerymen were the equals of any artillerymen in the A.E.F.[11]

In recognition of the historically effective service of the brigade, General Sherburne issued (excerpts from) the following General Oder dated February 3rd, 1919: "… the Brigade Commander wishes to record … the entire satisfaction it has given him to command the … first Brigade of Negro artillerymen ever organized. The satisfaction is due to the excellent record the men have made. Undertaking a work that was new to them, they brought to it faithfulness, zeal, and patriotic fervor. They went into the line and conducted themselves in a manner to win the praise of all … The Brigade Commander feels that he should also make an acknowledgement in the General Orders of the remarkable esprit-de-corps displayed by the officers of the brigade. They were pioneers in a field where, at the start, success was problematical. This being the first brigade of its kind ever organized, it has been only natural that the work of the men should have featured prominently, yet the same prominence and the same praise should be accorded the officers.[12]

With respect to the performance of the 92nd Division as a whole; General Pershing, at a January 28th 1919 review of the Division said: "… the 92nd Division stands second to none in the record you have made since your arrival in France.

This unidentified soldier posing in a studio in France wears a French bayonet on an unusual belt possibly bearing a Massachusetts or Virginia Militia belt plate. Courtesy Private Collection.

Captain Elijah Reynolds, 368th Infantry Regiment. Reynolds served as First Sergeant of Company F, 25th Infantry for thirty years. Courtesy Military History Institute.

Monument in German Grave Yard showing inscription "Ihren gefallenen Kameraden 1 Feld-Kompagnie Pionier Regiment no. 20." Colored soldier is Sergeant Avery Allen, Company D, 317th Engineers. France. Courtesy National Archives.

I am proud of the part you have played in the great conflict ... yet you have only done what the American people expected you to do and you have measured up to every expectation of the Commander-in-Chief ... I commend the 92nd Division for its achievements not only in the field, but on the record its men have made in their individual conduct. The American public has every reason to be proud of the record made by the 92nd Division.[13]

The Division's performance was not without its shortcomings. Some records are rather critical of the Division, advancing the arguments of those who embrace the theory that black combat units are inherently ineffective. While Major General Charles Ballou often praised the performance of his Division, in his last official communiqué to the Division, he hints of failures and disappointments. In his memorandum dated November 18th, 1918, he states: "... The Division Commander, in taking leave of what he considers his Division, feels that he has accomplished his mission. His work is done and will endure. The results have not always been brilliant, and many times were discouraging, yet a well organized, well disciplined and well trained colored Division has been created and commanded by him to include the last shot of the war."[14]

An unbiased look at the 92nd would not only reveal gallant and distinguished performance, sometimes under extraordinarily trying circumstances, but also significant internal problems that diminished the reputation of the Division. Reports from some officers and men indicate it was hamstrung by poor training, discrimination within the ranks, tension between black and white officers and a bitter feud between its' commander, Major General Charles Ballou and General Robert Bullard who commanded the U.S. Second Army to which the 92nd was attached.[15] In a September 1919 edition of the Messenger, two black officers, A.B. Nutt and William Colson described the 92nd Division as "a tragic failure." General Ballou himself at one point lamented, "It was my misfortune to be handicapped by many white officers who were rabidly hostile to the idea of a colored officer, and who continually conveyed misinformation to the staffs ... and generally created much trouble and discontent. Such men will never give the Negro the square deal that is

Testing masks, inspection by gas. 3rd Battalion, 366th Infantry Regiment in France. Courtesy National Archives.

Opposite: A lovely portrait of an unidentified 92nd Division soldier; he wears the division shoulder sleeve insignia and a pistol qualification badge. The photo is from a Richmond, Virginia estate. Courtesy Private Collection.

his just due."[16] The praises from General Pershing, accolades from the commanders of the Division, and their French Allies, the many awards and decorations earned by the Division and its' soldiers would, for several years, prove insufficient in overcoming the opinions that challenged the viability of a black fighting force.

Reference Bibliography:

General Division Histories:
American Battle Monuments Commission. *92nd Division, Summary of Operations in the World War.* Washington, DC: Government Printing Office, 1944.
Cochrane, Rexmond C. *The 92nd Division in the Marbache Sector, October 1918.* Army Chemical Center, MD: USA Chemical Corps History Office, 1959.
Scott, Emmett J. *The American Negro in World War I.* Emmet J. Scott, 1919
U.S. Army War College. Historical Section. "The Ninety-Second Division, 1917-1918." Study, 1923.

351st Field Artillery Regiment:
Ross, William O., Slaughter, Duke L. *With the 351st in France (A Diary).* Baltimore: Afro-American Company, 1919.

W.H. Cox, Color Sergeant, 15th New York Infantry [369th Regiment], Champagne 1918 by Raymond Desvarreaux,
Courtesy West Point Museum Art Collection, U.S. Military Academy

*C. Thompson, 15th New York Infantry [369th Regiment], Champagne 1918 by Raymond Desvarreaux, Courtesy
West Point Museum Art Collection, U.S. Military Academy*

Above: The Basketball Team of the 350th Field Artillery poses for the camera. The 350th Field Artillery was assigned to the 92nd Division. Courtesy Private Collection.

Opposite

Top: Non-commissioned Officers of the 92nd Division at bayonet training, I Corps School, Gondrecourt, France, August, 1918. Courtesy National Archives.

Bottom: Troops of the 92nd Division on the road near Binarville, France, October, 1918. Note the 77th Division insignia on the tailgate of the truck. Courtesy National Archives.

Colonel William Hayward, commander of the 369th Infantry Regiment playing baseball with his men, St. Nazaire, France, February, 1918. Of note is the National Guard designation of 15 NY on his overseas cap signifying the unit's original designation as the 15th Infantry Regiment, New York National Guard. Courtesy National Archives.

93rd Infantry Division (Colored)

The War Department established the 185th and 186th Brigades (Colored) on November 23, 1918 at Camp Stuart, Virginia. The 185th Brigade was composed of the 369th Infantry Regiment, the former 15th Infantry Regiment, New York National Guard, and the 370th Infantry, the former 8th Infantry Regiment, Illinois National Guard. The 186th Brigade was composed of the 371st Infantry Regiment, formed from African-American selective service men, and the 372nd Infantry Regiment, made up National Guard Units from Connecticut (1st Separate Company. Connecticut. Infantry), District of Columbia (1st Separate. Battalion). District of Columbia Infantry), Maryland (1st Separate Company Maryland Infantry), Massachusetts (1st Separate Company Massachusetts Infantry), Ohio (9th Separate Battalion Ohio Infantry), and Tennessee (1st Separate Company Tennessee Infantry). This division was never organized to its full strength, only the 185th and 186th Infantry Brigades being formed.[17]

Insignia

Originally, the division selected a red hand, the insignia of the French 157th Division, the French unit they served with. This alluded to the bloody hands of its soldiers from hand to hand combat. As this insignia was considered too graphic, the division was ordered to choose another insignia.[18] Then the division selected an insignia of a French Adrian helmet in light blue, superimposed on a black disc. The helmet symbolizes the service of the regiments with the French Divisions. The insignia was approved December 30, 1917. The subordinate regiments in this division adopted individual distinctive insignia: The 369th Infantry Regiment: a white snake with black markings upon a black square. The 372nd Infantry Regiment: A red hand bordered in blue on a khaki square. A number of variants of both the division and the regimental insignia exist.[19]

Campaigns:

Meuse-Argonne Offensive, 369th Infantry Regiment, Champagne Sector, Thur Sector, Vosges. 370th Infantry Regiment, Argonne Sector. 371st Infantry Regiment, Verdun Sector. 372nd Infantry Regiment, Argonne Sector.[20]

Division Organization (1917-1919):[21]

185th Infantry Brigade:
369th Infantry Regiment
370th Infantry Regiment

186th Infantry Brigade:
371st Infantry Regiment
372nd Infantry Regiment

Right: The standard insignia of the 93rd Division; a felt on felt French Helmet of horizon Blue material.

Far right: This variant uses die cut felt with a well worn velvet inset to form the design.

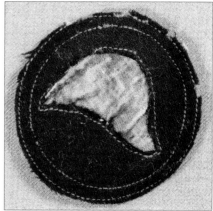

Far left: An embroidered on wool example of the 93rd Division insignia.

Left: This felt on felt variant of the 93rd Division insignia adds a helmet strap to the division design.

Right: Kid Ferguson, a star basketball player of the 369th Infantry Regiment at St. Nazaire, France, February, 1918. Note again the 15 designation on his overseas cap, and the NY 15 monogram on his singlet. Courtesy National Archives.

Far right: First Lieutenant Marc J. Logie of Company F, 372nd Infantry Regiment, Germany, 1919. Courtesy Military History Institute.

The 350th Field Artillery Regiment adopted their own insignia; this embroidered example features a white swastika with a blue dot at center upon a red background.

Their sister regiment, the 351st Field Artillery Regiment, also adopted the white swastika as their insignia substituting a red dot on a blue field.

The 369th Infantry Regiment, the Rattlesnake Regiment, adopted their own insignia; this embroidered white rattlesnake upon a back field is the standard pattern.

Division Combat Narrative:[22]

In compliance with War Department instructions organization of the 93rd Division was begun at Camp Stuart, Newport News, Virginia, in December, 1917. The nucleus of the division was composed of men from Connecticut, the District of Columbia, Illinois, Maryland, Massachusetts, New York, Ohio, Tennessee, and South Carolina.

The division was never fully organized, only headquarters and the 185th and 186th Infantry Brigades being formed. The Commanding General assumed command of the division at Camp Stuart, Newport News, Va., in December, 1917, at which time the infantry regiments of the organization were stationed at various widely separated posts in the United States.

Upon arrival in France headquarters was stationed at Bur-sur-Seine (Aube) pending the arrival and assembly of the units of the division. These units, however, consisting of the 369th, 370th, 371st and 372nd Infantry Regiments were brigaded with the French Army, and in May, 1918, the personnel of headquarters were attached to the 1st and 42nd Division pending the contemplated re-assembling of the 93rd Division. It was never re-assembled, although never formally dissolved, and its history therefore resolves itself into the histories of its four infantry regiments.

369th Infantry Regiment, Harlem Hellfighters or Rattlesnake Regiment.

This regiment was organized in April, 1917, as the 15th New York Infantry, a National Guard unit, but upon arrival in France it was designated as the 369th Infantry. The regiment arrived at Brest, December 26, 1917. Thence it moved to Saint Nazaire, January 1, 1918, remaining there until March 13, 1918, when it proceeded to Givry-en-Argonne. Upon arrival March 15, 1918, it was attached to the 16th Division, 8th Army Corps, 4th French Army, for purposes of instruction and training. Beginning April 8, 1918, the battalions of the regiment were successively placed in front line sector with French troops north of Saints-Monehould, in the Champagne. The regiment held this sector until July 5, 1918. It participated in the Champagne-Marne Defensive, July 15 to 19, 1918, in the Aisne-Marne Offensive, July 18 to 20, 1918, and in the offensive operations of the 4th French Army on the Champagne front, September 26 to 30, 1918. On October 14, 1918, the regiment, as part of the 161st Division, French, to which it has been assigned on July 15th, proceeded to Alsace. The battalions of the 369th Infantry took over sections of front line in the Vosges which they held until November 11, 1918. After the armistice the regiment became a part of the French Army of Occupation. On December 8, 1918, it was relieved from duty with the French Army, and proceeded to the Le Mans Embarkation Center preparatory to its return to the United States. The regiment sailed from Brest February 2, 1919, and arrived at New York February 12, 1919.

370th Infantry Regiment, the Black Devils.

This regiment was organized from the 8th Illinois (National Guard). It arrived in France in April, 1918, and trained with various French divisions until August 31, 1918, during which period detachments of the regiment were in front line positions. On September 15, 1918, the regiment as a part of the 59th Division, French, went into line in the Vauxaillon Area northeast of Soissons, and participated in the Oisen-Aisne Offensive, September 17 to October 12, 1918, and October 24 to November 11, 1918. The regiment embarked for the United States at Brest, February 1, 1919, and arrived at New York February 9, 1919.

371st Infantry Regiment, the Red Hand.

This regiment arrived in France in April, 1918, and as an independent unit of the 13th French Army Corps was in training from April 26 to June 6, 1918, in the vicinity of Bar-le-Duc. It joined the 68th Division, French, on June 13, 1918, in the vicinity of Verdun, remaining in support of this unit until June 22, 1918. From June 23 to September 14, 1918, the regiment was in line in the Verdun Sector. It participated in the offensive operations of the 4th French Army on the Champagne front September 27 to October 6, 1918, in the 157th Division, 9th French Army Corps. The 157th

Division was withdrawn from the line October 6, 1918, and proceeded to the Alsace Sector, Vosges. The regiment was in line in this Sector from October 16 to November 11, 1918. It was withdrawn November 15, 1918, and proceeded to the Le Mans Embarkation Center preparatory to returning to the United States. The regiment sailed from Brest February 3, 1919, and arrived at New York February 11, 1919.

The "Harlem Hellfighters" band of the 369th Infantry Regiment, leads the way on a road march in France, 1918. Bandleader Lieutenant James Reese Europe, an officer in the Machine Gun company marches to the right front of the band (left in photo). Courtesy National Archives.

372nd Infantry Regiment, The Red Hand.

This regiment arrived at Saint Nazaire, in April, 1918, and proceeded to the training center in the vicinity of Givry-en-Argonne for duty with the French Army. From June 6 to July 14, 1918, and from July 26 to September 9, 1918, the regiment was in line in the Argonne Sector. It participated in the offensive operations of the 4th French Army on the Champagne front September 26 to October 7, 1918, in the 157th Division, 9th French Army Corps. The regiment proceeded to the Vosges on October 11th where it occupied a sector of front from October 13, to November 11th. It remained in the Vosges until January 1, 1919, when it proceeded to the Le Mans Embarkation Center preparatory to returning to the United States. The regiment sailed from Brest on February 3, 1919, and arrived at New York on February 12, 1919.

The casualties of the four infantry regiments, 93rd Division, totaled 591 soldiers killed in action or died of wounds, 2,943 wounded in action.[23]

Although never fighting as a complete division, the division was assigned the famous 369th Infantry Regiment, the Harlem Hellfighters, or Rattlesnake Regiment

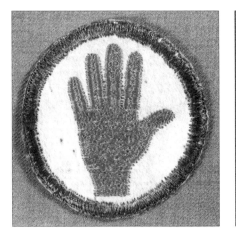

Far left: The 372nd Infantry Regiment adopted the original 93rd Division pattern, deemed too graphic by the AEF Headquarters, as their insignia; the embroidered Bloody Hand will forever be associated with the 372nd Infantry.

Left: Liberty Loan style Bloody Hand pattern 93rd Division insignia.

– the single most storied African-American regiment of World War I. The regimental band formed from prominent musicians, was led by Lieutenant James Reese Europe, and Drum Major Noble Sissle, and was instrumental in introducing jazz music to France. During World War I, no Medal of Honor was bestowed upon an African-American soldier. Subsequent action by the Army to review the policy at the time found that although several had been recommended for the award, they had been downgraded to the Distinguished Service Cross, with the exception of one soldier whose file was never acted upon. In 1991, Corporal Freddie Stowers, Company C, 371st Infantry Regiment was awarded the Medal of Honor posthumously for his actions in combat in 1918.

Reference Bibliography:

General Division Histories:
American Battle Monuments Commission. *93rd Division, Summary of Operations in the World War*. Washington, DC: Government Printing ,Office 1944.

Guttman, Jon. "Regiment's Pride." *Military History* (Oct 1991): pp. 35-41.

U.S. Congress, House of Representatives. *Erection of a Monument in France to Commemorate the Valiant Services of the Ninety-Third Division of the American Expeditionary Forces*. Hearings, 69th Congress, 1st session, Mar 1926.

—. Monument in France to Colored American Infantry Regiments Attached to the French Army. Report, 68th Congress, 2nd session, February 1925.

369th Infantry Regiment
Badger, Reid. *A Life in Ragtime: A Biography of James Reese Europe*. New York: Oxford, 1995.

Harris, Stephen L. *Harlem's Hell Fighters: The African-American 369th Infantry in World War I*. Washington, DC: Brassey's, 2003.

Harris, Bill. *The Hellfighters of Harlem: African-American Soldiers Who Fought for the Right to Fight for Their Country*. New York: Carroll & Graf, 2002.

Little, Arthur W. *From Harlem to the Rhine: The Story of New York's Colored Volunteers*. New York: Covici Friede, 1936.

Moore, William E., & Russell, James C. *U.S. Official Pictures of the World War: Showing America's Participation; Selected From the Official Files of the War Department*. 3 vols. n.p., Army & Navy Union, 1921.

371st Infantry Regiment
Beattie, Taylor V. "Corporal Freddie Stowers: An Appointment with Eternity on Hill 188." *Army History* (Winter 2003): pp. 14-20.

Beattie, Taylor V. "Seventy Three Years After his Bayonet Assault on Hill 188, Freddie Stowers Got His Medal of Honor." *Military History* (Aug 2004): pp. 74 and 76.

Deckard, Percy E. *List of Officers Who Served with the 371st Infantry and Headquarters, 186th Infantry Brigade during the World War*. Allegany, Pennsylvania: Allegany Citizen, 1929.

Heywood, Chester D. *List of Officers, 371st Infantry, World War I: A History*. n.p., nd.

—. *Negro Combat Troops in the World War: The Story of the 371st Infantry*. New York: 1928.

Scipio, L. Albert. *With the Red Hand Division*. Silver Springs, Maryland: Roman, 1985.

372nd Infantry Regiment
Mason, Monroe, & Furr, Arthur. *The American Negro Soldier with the Red Hand of France*. Boston: Cornhill, 1921.

Right: Church in Sector held by the 369th Infantry Regiment, 93rd Division, May 4, 1918. Courtesy National Archives.

Below: Colored troops in France 369th Infantry Regiment, 93rd Division in one of their camps, Maffrecourt, France. Courtesy National Archives.

This page: Colors of the 369th Infantry Regiment, 93rd Division, May 5, 1918. Courtesy National Archives.

Opposite

Top: Kitchen and dining quarters in trenches 369th Infantry Regiment. Courtesy National Archives.

Bottom: Mule drawn passenger car used between Regimental Headquarters and the Front. May 4, 1918. 369th Infantry Regiment, 93rd Division. Courtesy National Archives.

Opposite: Colonel William Hayward, commanding 369th Infantry Regiment, 93rd Division outside his dugout, sending message by carrier pigeon. Courtesy National Archives.

Right: Men of the 369th Infantry Regiment, 93rd Division amusing themselves with a one-round boxing bout. Maffrecourt, France. May 5, 1918. Courtesy National Archives.

Below: Supply train ready to leave for the Front. Maffrecourt, France. May 5, 1918. Courtesy National Archives.

A detachment of the 369th Infantry regiment in the trenches in France. Courtesy National Archives.

Above: Sentry box outside Regimental Headquarters 369th Infantry, 93rd Division. Notice horn for gas attack and camouflage gate. May 4, 1918. Also note French soldier at extreme right. Courtesy National Archives.

Opposite
Top: One reason [the American food] why the men were glad to get back to the 93rd Division. Note the 93rd Division Patches these men are wearing. Courtesy National Archives.

Bottom: 1st Lieutenant James R. Europe, of the 369th Regiment Infantry, playing for the patients of Hospital Number 9. Sergeant Wood Andress is the first musician on the right and plays the slide trombone. American Red Cross Hospital Number 9. Paris, France, September 4, 1918. Courtesy National Archives.

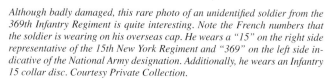

Although badly damaged, this rare photo of an unidentified soldier from the 369th Infantry Regiment is quite interesting. Note the French numbers that the soldier is wearing on his overseas cap. He wears a "15" on the right side representative of the 15th New York Regiment and "369" on the left side indicative of the National Army designation. Additionally, he wears an Infantry 15 collar disc. Courtesy Private Collection.

Right: A portrait of a returning member of the 93rd Division (note divisional shoulder sleeve insignia on his left shoulder); the photographer etched into the photo, "Just From France." Courtesy Private Collection.

Opposite: Jewel Crawford, Company H, 369th Infantry Regiment, stands in his yard after returning from the war. He holds a Trapdoor Springfield, a relic of an earlier war, but manages a martial look. Courtesy Private Collection.

The 369th Infantry Regiment, the Harlem Hellfighters on board the S.S. Stockholm, just home from France February 9, 1919. Jewell Crawford can be seen second from the left, smiling and wearing a mustache. Courtesy Private Collection.

Opposite: George Biggs and George Vernall sat for this photo in New Haven, Connecticut in 1919. Biggs was assigned to Company M, 372nd Infantry Regiment. Note the Red Hand shoulder sleeve insignia on his uniform. Courtesy Private Collection.

In this important and never before published series of seven photos, we witness a concert by the 369th Infantry Regiment Band; in the first in the series, Drum Major and vocalist Noble Sissle faces the crowd, singing, the dignitaries have not yet arrived, they are late for the concert – a nun snaps a photo; Lieutenant Europe stands directly behind her directing the band. Courtesy Private Collection.

Opposite
Top: Lieutenant Europe prepares to start a number; several soldiers turn to look at the photographer. Courtesy Private Collection.

Bottom: French and American dignitaries rise for the playing of the National Anthems. Courtesy Private Collection.

Lieutenant James Reese Europe conducts as the members play. Notice the numbers "369" on the overseas cap of the soldier to the left. Courtesy Private Collection.

As the band plays, several band members perform a dance routine. Courtesy Private Collection.

The "Percussion Twins," Herbert and Steve Wright, finish out the concert. Herbert Wright would brutally murder James Europe on the evening of May 9, 1919 as a result of a perceived slight after a concert in Boston. Courtesy Private Collection.

Noble Sissle ends the concert. Courtesy Private Collection.

CHAPTER THREE

NEGRO OFFICERS FOR THE ARMY

Opposite
Top left: A pre-war military song sheet entitled "Ole South, Plantation March" depicting the stereotypical view of the black man. Black Americans wishing to contribute to the war effort needed to overcome these prejudicial views. Courtesy Military History Institute.

Top right: After political pressure from Congress, the War Department acquiesced to the inclusion of black soldiers. This official poster uses the iconic image of Lincoln as the Great Emancipator now proud of the accomplishment of the black soldier. This poster resulted in thousands of black men answering the country's call to service. Courtesy Military History Institute.

Center: "Good Bye Alexander" is another song in this genre. It celebrates the departure of black fighters overseas. Courtesy Military History Institute.

Bottom left: "My Choc'late Soldier Sammy Boy" was written for the families of black soldiers. Tin Pan Alley produced hundreds of songs of this genre for white soldiers – black themed soldier songs are uncommon. A Sammy was the World War I term for a "GI" – one of Uncle Sam's soldiers. Courtesy Military History Institute.

Bottom right: The song sheet, "You'll Find Old Dixieland in France" tells of the arrival of our black soldiers in France and the promise of their future deeds. Courtesy Military History Institute.

With the War Department's final acceptance of black soldiers for the expanded Army, it only followed that some would raise the question of commissioning black officers. Emmitt J. Scott noted in his book that:

"Congress authorized the establishment of a number of training camps for white officers, the number to be left to the discretion of the Secretary of War. No provision was made for the training of colored officers. After repeated efforts of various kinds, a committee composed of representative citizens, headed by Dr. Joel E. Spingarn[1] of New York City, held a conference with the military authorities. The efforts of the committee were fruitless for the time being, at least, and the committee was dissolved. The project was later taken up by the students of Howard University together with a few members of the faculty and students from other colleges, from Lincoln University, Fisk University, Atlanta University, Morehouse College, Tuskegee Normal and Industrial Institute, Hampton Agricultural and Industrial Institute, Virginia Union Seminary, and Morgan College."

Scott continues:

"Dr. Joel E. Spingarn consulted General Leonard Wood, who was at this time in charge of the Eastern Department, Governor's Island, New York, about the establishment of a "Plattsburg" for colored men. General Wood gave assurance that the same aid and assistance could be given a camp for colored men that were given the camp for white men, provided 200 men of college grade could be secured. Dr. Spingarn set out upon a vigorous campaign, sending letters and circulars in every direction and personally visiting Howard University and kindred institutions. Success crowned his indefatigable industry, but not without great opposition.

Dr. Spingarn's efforts, by many of the important newspapers and leaders of the race, were referred to as being designed to bring about the establishment of a "Jim Crow Camp" for training colored officers. The agitation grew quite violent at times, particularly because of the fact that Dr. Spingarn was Chairman of the Executive Committee of the National Association for the Advancement of Colored People, an organization generally regarded as standing uncompromisingly for the rights of the Negro people. In his efforts to secure the establishment of this camp Dr. Spingarn had the cooperation of his aide, Dr. W.E.B. DuBois, Editor of *The Crisis,* also regarded as an uncompromising champion of the Negro,

and of Col. Charles Young, United States Army, and such virile speakers and leaders as William Pickens and others. The agitation among the Negro group and the recognized friends of the Negro grew so warm that for a while divided counsels threatened the establishment of a camp. Whether through a fortunate or unfortunate turn of circumstances, while this agitation was at its height, Congress declared that a state of war existed between the United States and the Imperial German Government. Immediately, civilian training camps were abolished and fourteen Government camps were established for the training of officers."

When the War Department created fourteen training camps for white officers only, denying any opportunity for the commissioning of black officers, Scott realized that his best option was to take the case directly to Congress, thus pressuring the War Department from above. He formed a "Central Committee of Negro College Men" which began mobilizing for the campaign by collecting signatures black college students willing to serve in the Army. Then he had cards dropped off on the desks of members of congress which stated:

TRAINING CAMP FOR NEGRO OFFICERS

Our country faces the greatest crisis in its history; the Negro, as ever, loyal and patriotic, is anxious to do his full share in the defense and support of his country in its fight for democracy. The Negro welcomes the opportunity of contributing his full quota to the Federal army now being organized. He feels very strongly that these Negro troops should be officered by their own men. The following statement presents the facts upon which we base our request for an officers' reserve training camp for Negroes.

1 (a) Fourteen officers' training camps are to be opened on May 14, 1917, to provide officers for the new Federal Army.

(b) No officers are to be commissioned unless they receive training in one of these fourteen training camps:

(c) The War Department has stated that it is impracticable to admit Negroes to the fourteen established camps.

2 (a) The Negro is to furnish his proportionate quota in this army,

Fort Des Moines, Iowa; it was here that the first commissioning class for black officers was held. Courtesy National Archives.

View of Fort Des Moines, Iowa as seen from the west. Courtesy Military History Institute.

(b) It seems just that the competent and intelligent Negroes should have the opportunity to lead these troops;

(e) One thousand Negro college students and graduates have already pledged themselves to enter such a training camp immediately;

(d) In addition men in the medical profession desire to qualify for service in the Medical Corps, and there are other competent men ready to qualify for other specialized corps provided for;

(e) Records of Negro officers and troops warrant the provision for Negro officers to lead Negro troops.

Lieutenant General Young, Major Loving, Captain Davis, Major Walker

3. Therefore, the Negro race requests the establishment of an officers' reserve training camp for Negroes.

CENTRAL COMMITTEE OF NEGRO COLLEGE MEN.

Signed:

FRANK COLEMAN, Chicago,.	T.M. GREGORY, Harvard,
W. DOUGLAS, Lincoln,	C.H. HOUSTON, Amherst,
W.A. HALL, Union,	L.H. RUSSELL, Cornell,
M.H. CURTIS, Howard,	C.B. CURLEY, General Secretary,
Howard University, Washington, D.C."	

Scott's efforts paid off, over 300 Senators and Representatives approved of the idea and Congressional inquiries began pouring in to the War Department. Scott coupled his Congressional campaign with an information campaign to the press. A sample press release read:

"THE COLORED PEOPLE OF THE COUNTRY MAKING STRENUOUS EFFORTS TO SECURE TRAINING CAMP FOR COLORED OFFICERS."

Headquarters and Recruiting Station at Howard University.
"According to the best authorities about 83,000 Negroes will be drafted for the New Federal Army. The Negroes welcome this opportunity of serving their country, and sharing their full responsibilities in this time of national peril. They feel, however, that Negro troops thus raised should be officered by men of their own race and are making strenuous efforts to secure a training camp in which such officers can be prepared. The War Department has stated that it is impracticable to admit Negroes to the fourteen camps for officers to be opened on May 14, 1917. And it has also stated that no officers are to be commissioned unless they receive training in one of these camps. This means that unless some provision is made whereby colored men may be trained for officers these 83,000 Negro troops

will be officered exclusively by white officers; and that Negroes qualified both mentally and physically to serve as officers will be forced under the conscription law to serve as privates. The colored man is willing and ready to carry out the duties imposed upon him as an American citizen, and feels that he should be given the same opportunities in the performance of these duties as are given to other American citizens. The Negroes from every section are requesting that the Government provide means whereby colored officers may be trained. The appeal is just, reasonable, and practicable. The proposition is squarely up to the Government. This is no time for sectional differences and race prejudice and the highest patriotism demands that every American citizen be given the opportunity to serve his country in the capacity for which he is best fitted. Over one thousand colored men have sent their names to their headquarters at Howard University, and hundreds of others are arriving by mail and telegrams. Why should not colored troops be officered by colored men? Their records show them to be competent and efficient, and to deny any class of citizens the opportunity of rendering its best service belies the very theory of our democracy, and the basic principle for which the present war is waged. Our American statesmen should frown upon any procedure that does not offer an equal opportunity for all at all times, but more especially at a time when our country is faced by a foreign foe."

On May 12, 1917, the War Department relented and announced a plan to establish a camp for Negro officers. "The authorization of the camp brought joy unspeakable to the hearts of the committee and students. Smiles and handshakes soon made the campus seem like an old-fashioned Methodist prayer meeting and the news was heralded far and wide."

Scott states that:

"As a result of these persistent efforts a training camp for colored officers was authorized by the Secretary of War on the 19th of May and soon thereafter the candidates for commissions set out for Fort Des Moines, Iowa, where they were to undergo training. The Honorable Champ Clark, Speaker of the House of Representatives, said that this marked "an epoch in American history and a new day for the Negro."

He goes on to say:

"The student officers were put through weeks of intensive training under Col. C.C. Ballou, his staff, and a group of colored noncommissioned officers from the four colored regiments of the Regular Army. The Presidents and other officers of the various colored institutions of learning whose officers, teachers and students were in training visited the camp and spoke to the officer-candidates. Dr. George W. Cabannis, a colored physician of Washington, D.C., voluntarily gave up his practice and enlisted in the Y.M.C.A. work as a Secretary, and took charge of the Y.M.C.A. tent at Ft. Des Moines, working in closest cooperation with Col. Ballou and his military aides. It was expected that the training would last three months. At the end of that period, however, the War Department decided to continue training for another month. Suspicion became rife among the men; many of them dropped out, giving as a reason that "the War Department never intended to commission colored men as officers in the army." There were only a few of those faint-hearted fellows, however; the great majority remained, and on October 14, 1917, Col. W.T. Johnson of the Adjutant General's Office arrived at Ft. Des Moines with commissions for 639 officers, 106 captains; 329 first lieutenants, and 204 second lieutenants. On that day, October 14, 1917, amidst impressive ceremonies, the 17th Provisional Training Regiment, as the Fort Des Moines Training Camp was called, was formed on the drill-ground facing the Administration building; here with bared heads and uplifted hands these 639 members of the regiment (the unsuccessful

Opposite: A Christmas 1918 photograph of Second Lieutenant Joseph L. Johnson of Philadelphia, Pennsylvania. Johnson was commissioned on October 15, 1917 at Fort Des Moines, Iowa as part the first black officer training course conducted by the 17th Provisional Training Regiment. Courtesy Private Collection.

View of Joseph Johnson while attending the camp. Courtesy Private Collection.

members having been dismissed) took the solemn oath which was administered by Col. Johnson, Chief of the Division of Training Camps, War Department. On the next day, October 15, the successful candidates received commissions and were ordered to report after fifteen days' leave of absence to their respective camps. In equally divided groups the 639 officers were sent to the following camps, reporting for duty on the 1st of November, 1917: Camp Funston, Kansas; Camp Dodge, Iowa; Camp Grant, Illinois; Camp Sherman, Ohio Camp Meade, Maryland; Camp Dix, New Jersey; Camp Upton, New York. It was at these widely distributed camps that the various units of the 92nd Division (the authorized colored Division) were trained. Some of the difficulties which befell the 92nd Division are to be ascribed to the fact that the units of the Division were never united until they reached France, being trained in the seven camps here mentioned; this was true of no other division of the army sent overseas."

In addition to the officer training camp at Des Moines, the War Department eventually established several Student Army Training Detachments (SATC) for blacks. These detachments became were active on October 1, 1918.

Detachments were divided into two sections: colligate sections and vocational sections. Colligate students with appropriate academic achievement had the opportunity to pursue commissions; students in vocational sections received two months of vocational and academic training with an opportunity to receive two additional months of advanced training if they demonstrated acceptable grades. At the completion of training, colligate students could enroll in the Central Officer's Training School which produced non-commissioned officers or continue into advanced college programs. Vocational section graduates could be assigned to Vocational Training Sections or would report for duty in the Army as privates. Either way, this program offered for black soldiers unique opportunities to better themselves.[2]

Vocational Sections were established at Tuskegee Institute, Hampton Institute, Howard University, Atlanta University, Georgia State Agricultural and Mechanical College, Agricultural and Technical College of North Carolina, Prairie View Normal School, Lincoln University, Chester County, Pennsylvania, West Virginia Collegiate Institute, Wilberforce University, Alabama State A&M College, Tennessee A&I College, Louisiana A&M College

Collegiate Sections were established at: Howard, Lincoln University at Chester, Pennsylvania, Fisk University, Meharry Medical College, Talladega College, Virginia Union University and Wilberforce.

Combined Sections were established at Atlanta and Morehouse College and Wiley College and Bishop College.

Additionally, the War Department opened SATC Detachments with advanced college programs at the following universities:

Howard University, Washington, D.C.
Howard was established on March 2, 1867 under a charter enacted by Congress, the college was named after General Oliver Otis Howard who was commissioner of the Freedmen's Bureau and the college's third president. Howard was often the center of early efforts to better the cause of Black Americans and as such, was a natural selection as a test bed for Army educational programs.

Tuskegee Institute, Tuskegee, Alabama.
The school was the dream of Lewis Adams, a former slave and George W. Campbell, a former slave owner. Booker T. Washington was the first head of the school and resultant of his efforts, by the outbreak of World War I, Tuskegee Institute had become a respected institution for the education of black Americans.

Western University, Quindaro, Kansas.
Western University at Quindaro, Kansas, was probably the earliest black school west of the Mississippi and the best black musical training center in the Midwest for almost thirty years during the 1900s through the 1920s.

An unidentified but dashing officer in a striking portrait. Courtesy Private Collection.

A stunning portrait of an unidentified officer, possibly Captain Arthur C. Newman, from a Richmond, Virginia estate; note the District of Columbia World War I service medal. Courtesy Private Collection.

A 1917 group photograph of the Officers of Company C, 366th Infantry Regiment at Camp Dodge, Iowa. Sitting (from right to left) Lieutenant John F. Rice, Lieutenant Earl W. Mann, Captain Emmitt White, Lieutenant Clifford W. Jones, (from right to left standing) Lieutenant Ralph E. Mizell, Lieutenant James L. Elliott, Lieutenant Marshall Meadows. All of these men graduated from the 17th Provisional Training regiment Colored Officer Class and were commissioned at Fort Des Moines on October 15, 1917. The 366th Infantry Regiment would be assigned to the 92nd Division in France. Courtesy Private Collection.

Prairie View Normal School, Prairie View, Texas
Prairie View Normal School was founded as a land grant college in 1876 and quickly established a reputation for producing black educators.

Branch Normal College, Pine Bluff, Arkansas
Branch Normal College was founded in 1873. It was nominally part of the "normal" (education) department of Arkansas Industrial University, later the University of Arkansas, but was operated separately due to segregation. It later became a land-grant college under the 1890 amendments to Morrill Land-Grant Colleges Act, which required states which did not open their land-grant university to all races to establish a separate land-grant university for each race.

Hampton Institute, Hampton, Virginia
Hampton Institute can trace its roots to the work of Mary S. Peake of Norfolk which began in 1861 with outdoor classes taught under the landmark Emancipation Oak in the nearby area of Elizabeth City County adjacent to the old sea port of Hampton. The newly-issued Emancipation Proclamation was first read to a gathering under this Oak Tree.

In 1868, a normal school was formalized with former Union Brigadier General Samuel C. Armstrong as its first principal. The new school was established as "Hampton Normal and Agricultural Institute."

Among Hampton's earliest students was Booker T. Washington, who arrived from West Virginia in 1872 at the age of sixteen. He worked his way through Hampton, and then went on to attend Wayland Seminary in Washington D.C. After graduation there, he returned to Hampton and became a teacher.

Negro Agricultural and Technical College, Greensboro, North Carolina
The North Carolina Agricultural and Technical State University was established under the Second Morrill Act; it was passed by Congress on August 30, 1890 and by an act of the General Assembly of North Carolina. Ratification was on March 9, 1891.

Below: A group of unknown officers poses together for the camera. Courtesy Private Collection.

The college was named the "A and M College for the Colored Race." Following the language of the first Morrill Act, the state law specifically declared that, "the leading objective of the college shall be to teach practical agriculture and the mechanic arts and such learning as related thereto, not excluding academic and classical instruction." The "A&M College for the Colored Race" was located on the campus of Shaw University in Raleigh, NC for three years (1891-1893), and was known as Shaw Annex Program. Female students were a part of the college from 1893 until 1901, but were not enrolled again until 1928. The college had numerous name changes. In 1915, the name was changed from the "A and M College for the Colored Race" to the "Negro Agricultural and Technical College of North Carolina."

Atlanta University, Atlanta, Georgia
Atlanta University, founded in 1865, by the American Missionary Association, with later assistance from the Freedman's Bureau, was, before consolidation, the nation's oldest graduate institution serving a predominantly African American student body. By the late 1870s, Atlanta University had begun granting bachelor's degrees and supplying black teachers and librarians to the public schools of the South.

Wilberforce University, Xenia, Ohio
Wilberforce University was founded in 1856 by a Black bishop, Bishop Daniel Paine of the National Methodist Episcopal Church. The college closed temporarily in 1862 during the American Civil War. The following year it reopened after being sold to the African Methodist Episcopal Church.

Opposite: This young unidentified officer's photo came from a Virginia estate. Courtesy Private Collection.

Lieutenant Robert Johnson is resplendent before the camera; he was a longtime trustee at a one room school in Blacksburg, Virginia. Courtesy Private Collection.

South Carolina Agricultural and Mechanical College, Orangeburg, South Carolina

Founded under the Morrill Land Grant Act, the South Carolina General Assembly created the Colored, Normal, Industrial, Agricultural, and Mechanical College of South Carolina on March 3, 1896. The new school, separated from nearby Claflin College. For twenty-four years, the school operated in one building, Morrill Hall, which held classrooms, the library, dormitories, and the president's office and residence.

Fiske University, Nashville, Tennessee

Fisk was established by John Ogden, Reverend Erastus Milo Cravath and Reverend Edward P. Smith and named in honor of General Clinton B. Fisk of the Tennessee Freedmen's Bureau. Fisk opened to classes on January 9, 1866. The world-famous Fisk Jubilee Singers started as a group of students who traveled to earn enough money to save the school and to raise funds to build the first permanent structure in the country built for the education of newly freed slaves. They succeeded and funded construction of the renowned Jubilee Hall.

CHAPTER FOUR

THE REGULAR ARMY UNITS AND COLORED TROOPS IN THE STATES

Every American soldier's service during World War I began in the United States where huge camps of instruction sprung up before the war to support the expansion of the Army. Prior to the National Defense Act of 1916, many of these camps were used by the National Guard and Militia. Some of these camps had served as staging areas for the Expedition to Mexico.

Regular Army units were recruited in the states and then shipped off to their respective units. National Guard and National Army units would begin their service in the many of the new cantonment areas built during the unprecedented expansion of the Army. Many black soldiers trained at these stateside camps would remain in the States working in supporting roles. As with the black soldiers who found themselves shipped overseas with the American Expeditionary Forces, most were relegated to labor tasks.

Black Regular Army Units

After the American Civil War, the War Department moved to increase the size of the Regular Army, resourcing fifty percent of the increase from black men. In 1866 eight new infantry regiments were authorized, of which four were black. They were the 38th, 39th, 40th and 41st Infantry Regiments. Additionally, four new cavalry regiments were recruited, of which two were black. They were the 9th and 10th Cavalry Regiments. In 1869 a reduction in the Regular Army prompted a consolidation of the infantry regiments. The 38th and 41st were combined to form the 24th Infantry Regiment. The 39th and 40th were consolidated into the 25th Infantry Regiment. The strength and designation of the cavalry regiments remained unchanged.[1]

When America declared war on Imperial Germany, there were some 20,000 trained and experienced black Soldiers currently in service. About 10,000 were in the ranks of the four Regular Army Regiments (9th and 10th Cavalry Regiments and the 24th and 25th Infantry Regiments). The remainder manned the ranks of National Guard Regiments, Separate Battalions and Companies. It was through these National Guard elements and black draftees that the War Department sought to enlist the service of black Americans for active participation in the Great War. The famed and experienced Regular Army Regiments were assigned other important missions, but would not see service in Europe.[2]

The 9th Cavalry Regiment served America's interests at Stotsenburg Camp in Luzon, Philippines. However, twenty-five members attended the black officer training camp at Fort Des Moines, Iowa. Twenty-one were awarded commissions; the majority of these were assigned to service and training battalions.

The 10th Cavalry Regiment was garrisoned at Fort Huachuca near Tombstone, Arizona. Their duties included patrolling the U.S.-Mexican border. On occasion, they were actively engaged in putting down uprisings on the Mexican side. Not all of the 10th Cavalry's Soldiers remained with the unit. More than sixty-six non-commissioned officers became officers in other units, and about 600 experienced men were graduated into the noncommissioned officer ranks, some serving with the 10th Cavalry, others assigned to different units.

The 24th Infantry Regiment, having recently rendered gallant service with General Pershing during the Punitive Expedition in 1916, was assigned to patrol duties along the Mexican-American border.

The 25th Infantry Regiment was garrisoned at Schofield Barracks, Hawaii. However, in 1918, they were returned to the Continental United States to perform border patrol duties along the Mexican-American border, thereby freeing a white regiment for service in France. Nonetheless, some eighty black noncommissioned officers were sent to Fort Des Moines, Iowa, where they were trained and commissioned as lieutenants. These officers then served with labor and training units during the War. They were reverted back to noncommissioned officers and returned to the 25th after the War. In total, greater than 1,000 men from the both the 24th and 25th Infantry Regiments became specialists and noncommissioned officers, and many did in fact attend officers training and were commissioned.

A private in B Company, 24th Infantry Regiment simply identified on the photograph by his first name, "Spencer," poses for a studio portrait. Courtesy Private Collection.

Opposite: This magnificent color tinted portrait of a soldier in the 3rd Battalion, 25th Infantry Regiment with two years overseas service, as illustrated by his four six-month overseas service chevrons, probably for service at Schofield Barracks, Hawaiian Territory. The medal is most likely a Mexican Border Service medal. Courtesy Private Collection.

An unknown 24th Infantry Regiment Sergeant poses on the Border with a cigarette. Courtesy Private Collection.

A soldier wearing a 25th Infantry Regiment collar insignia stands in front of a billet in France. Courtesy Private Collection.

A prewar view of a 24th Infantry Regiment soldier shows him in his dress uniform. Men like this one formed the non-commissioned officer cadre for both the 92nd and 93rd Divisions. Courtesy Private Collection.

Congregational Group, September 3, 1918, Camp Zachary Taylor, Louisville, Kentucky. (Reverend) Frederick B. Withington (seated second from left, front row) during Chaplain's training August – September 1918; Withington was commissioned as a chaplain in the 29th Division. Note that in this rare photo, the class contains an unidentified black chaplain candidate. This may well be photographic evidence of the first example of a racially integrated training class predating President Truman's landmark Executive Order by over thirty years. Courtesy Military History Institute.

Stateside Units

The following is a comprehensive listing of units in the States in which black soldiers served. The information which follows is drawn from a War Department report compiled from the Rolls and Rosters Section of the Adjutant Generals Office, the Returns Section Adjutant General Office and Organizational Directory, of the United States Army, 1919, and Historical Section Correspondence File Number 1957.

Engineers[3]

Engineer Service Battalions consisted of a Headquarters Detachment, four companies and a Medical Department with an aggregate strength of 1,040 men. Each of the companies had three officers and 250 soldiers and was equipped with one ½ ton motor truck, two two-ton motor trucks, a water cart and two motorcycles with sidecar and was designed to accomplish a variety of labor related tasks including bridging, road construction/repair, and other general engineering tasks.[4]

551st Engineer Service Battalion. The battalion was organized in October 1918 at Camp Humphreys, Virginia where it remained until it was demobilized in January 1919.

552nd Engineer Service Battalion. The battalion was organized in October 1918 at Camp Humphreys, Virginia where it remained until it was demobilized in January 1919.

553rd Engineer Service Battalion. The battalion was organized in October 1918 at Camp Humphreys, Virginia where it remained until it was demobilized in January 1919.

A Volleyball Game at Camp Wadsworth, South Carolina; Herman Zapf shot this picture of the white soldiers from the Cooks and Bakers School playing against "the Shines." From his photographic album dated 1918. Courtesy Military History Institute.

554th Engineer Service Battalion. The battalion was organized in October 1918 at Camp Humphreys, Virginia where it remained until it was demobilized in November 1918.

556th Engineer Service Battalion. The battalion was organized in October 1918 at Camp Humphreys, Virginia where it remained until it was demobilized in November 1918.

564th Engineer Service Battalion. The battalion was organized in November 1918 at Camp Shelby, Mississippi where it remained until it was demobilized in December 1918.

565th Engineer Service Battalion. The battalion was organized in October 1918 at Camp Shelby, Mississippi where it remained until it was demobilized in December 1918.

566th Engineer Service Battalion. The battalion was organized in October 1918 at Camp Shelby, Mississippi where it remained until it was demobilized in December 1918.

567th Engineer Service Battalion. The battalion was organized in October 1918 at Camp Wheeler, Georgia where it remained until it was demobilized in December 1918.

Pioneer Infantry[5]

A Pioneer Infantry Regiment had an aggregate strength of 3,551 men. It was composed of a headquarters and headquarters company, a supply company, three infantry battalions, a medical department and chaplains. Each battalion consisted of a headquarters and four companies. Each Pioneer infantry company consisted of six officers and 250 men. The Regiment was equipped with fourteen four-mule combat wagons, twenty four-mule ration and baggage wagons, thirty-eight bicycles and two motorcycles with sidecars. In addition to being trained as infantrymen, the unit was trained to perform routine labor tasks including roadwork, general construction, and fortification construction.[6]

6th Pioneer Infantry Regiment. The regiment was organized at Camp Sherman, Ohio in October 1918 where it remained until it was demobilized in February 1919. The regiment was commanded by Captain J.B. Babcock.

60th Pioneer Infantry Regiment. The regiment was organized at Camp Wadsworth, South Carolina in July 1918 where it remained until it was demobilized in January 1919.

Right: The cover of this Souvenir Folder illustrates a break in training at Camp Pike, Arkansas where many black soldiers received their initial training. Courtesy Military History Institute.

Below: Open air entertainment for the soldiers of Camp Pike by the "All Star" Plantation Musical Organization of the Colored Officers Trainees. Courtesy Military History Institute.

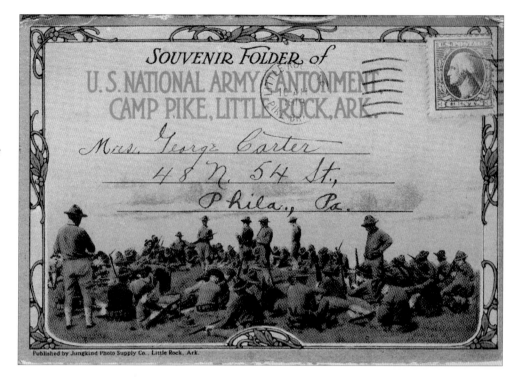

View of Piers Number 5 and 6, Newport News, Virginia; many of the black soldiers bound from Europe left from these docks. Courtesy National Archives.

61st Pioneer Infantry Regiment. The regiment was organized at Camp Wadsworth, South Carolina in July 1918 where it remained until it was demobilized in January 1919.

63rd Pioneer Infantry Regiment. The regiment was organized at Camp Dix, New Jersey in October 1918 where it remained until it was demobilized in January 1919.

64th Pioneer Infantry Regiment. The regiment was organized at Camp Zachery Taylor, Kentucky in October 1918 where it remained until it was demobilized in February 1919.

65th Pioneer Infantry Regiment. The regiment was organized at Camp Funston, Kansas in October 1918 where it remained until it was demobilized in December 1918.

810th Pioneer Infantry Regiment. The regiment was organized at Camp Greene, North Carolina in September 1918; the unit remained at Camp Greene until they were demobilized. The unit was commanded by Colonel W. A. Kent.

812th Pioneer Infantry Regiment. The regiment was organized at Camp Grant, Illinois in August 1918; the unit moved to Camp Merritt, New Jersey in November 1918 and remained there until it was returned to Camp Grant where it was demobilized in January 1919. The unit was commanded by Colonel F. Chamberlain.

Service Battalions (Formerly Reserve Labor Battalions)[7]
A Service Battalion had an aggregate strength of 1,248 with seventeen white officers, forty-eight white soldiers and 1,183 black soldiers. It consisted of a headquarters, four companies and a medical department. The unit was equipped with two motor trucks, one water cart and two motorcycles per company.[8] Farrow defined Labor Companies as "Colored troops attached to the Quartermasters' Department for special Services."[9] These units were used for a variety of labor needs by the Army.

350th Reserve Service Battalion. The battalion was organized in October 1918 at Camp Greene, North Carolina where it remained until it was demobilized in March 1919.

351st Reserve Service Battalion. The battalion was organized in October 1918 at Camp Greene, North Carolina where it remained until it was demobilized in January 1919.

352nd Reserve Service Battalion. The battalion was organized in October 1918 at Camp Greene, North Carolina where it remained until it was demobilized in January 1919.

353rd Reserve Service Battalion. The battalion was organized in October 1918 at Camp Greene, North Carolina where it remained until it was demobilized in January 1919.

354th Reserve Service Battalion. The battalion was organized in October 1918 at Camp Greene, North Carolina where it remained until it was demobilized in January 1919.

355th Reserve Service Battalion. The battalion was organized in October 1918 at Camp Alexander, Virginia in December 1918, it moved to New Cumberland, Pennsylvania where it remained until it was demobilized in April 1919.

356th – 400th Reserve Service Battalion. Never Organized.

401st Reserve Service Battalion. The battalion was organized in September 1918 at Camp Eustis, Virginia where it remained until it was demobilized in April 1919.

402nd Reserve Service Battalion. The battalion was organized in June 1918 at Camp Hancock, Georgia where it remained until it was demobilized in March 1919.

403rd Reserve Service Battalion. The battalion was organized in June 1918 at Camp Wheeler, Georgia where it remained until it was demobilized in March 1919.

404th Reserve Service Battalion. The battalion was organized in July 1918 at Camp Hill, Virginia where it remained until it was demobilized in August 1919.

405th Reserve Service Battalion. The battalion was organized in May 1918 at Newport News, Virginia where it remained until it was demobilized at Camp Hill, Virginia in August 1919.

406th Reserve Service Battalion. The battalion was organized in July 1918 at Camp Gordon, Georgia where it remained until it was demobilized in September 1919.

407th Reserve Service Battalion. The battalion was organized in August 1918 at Camp Lee, Virginia where it remained until it was demobilized in September 1919.

408th Reserve Service Battalion. The battalion was organized in July 1918 at Camp Jackson, South Carolina where it remained until it was demobilized in July 1919.

409th Reserve Service Battalion. The battalion was organized in September 1918 at Camp Pike, Arkansas where it remained until it was demobilized in June 1919.

410th Reserve Service Battalion. The battalion was organized in August 1918 at Camp MacArthur, Texas where it remained until it was demobilized in March 1919.

411th Reserve Service Battalion. The battalion was organized in August 1918 at Camp Zachary Taylor, Kentucky where it remained until it was demobilized in September 1919.

412th Reserve Service Battalion. The battalion was organized in September 1918 at Camp Travis, Texas where it remained until it was demobilized in April 1919.

413th Reserve Service Battalion. The battalion was organized in August 1918 at Camp Dix, New Jersey where it remained until it was demobilized in July 1919.

414th Reserve Service Battalion. The battalion was organized in August 1918 at Camp Dodge, Iowa where it remained until it was demobilized in July 1919.

Interior of Pier Number 4, Port of Embarkation, Newport News, Virginia. Courtesy National Archives.

The gate of Camp Pike, Arkansas from a book of Scenes of Camp Pike, National Army Cantonment, Little Rock, Arkansas. Courtesy Military History Institute.

415th Reserve Service Battalion. The battalion was organized in August 1918 at Camp Funston, Kansas where it remained until it was demobilized in September 1919.

416th Reserve Service Battalion. The battalion was organized in July 1918 at Camp Grant, Illinois where it remained until it was demobilized in May 1919.

417th Reserve Service Battalion. The battalion was organized in September 1918 at Camp Meade, Maryland where it remained until it was demobilized in June 1919.

418th Reserve Service Battalion. The battalion was organized in August 1918 at Camp Sherman, Ohio where it remained until it was demobilized in September 1919.

419th Reserve Service Battalion. The battalion was organized in August 1918 at Camp Beauregard, Louisiana where it remained until it was demobilized in March 1919.

420th Reserve Service Battalion. The battalion was organized in July 1918 at Camp Shelby, Mississippi where it remained until it was demobilized in September 1919.

421st Reserve Service Battalion. The battalion was organized in October 1918 at Camp Sheridan, Alabama where it remained until it was demobilized in March 1919.

422nd Reserve Service Battalion. The battalion was organized in August 1918 at Camp Wadsworth, South Carolina where it remained until it was demobilized in March 1919.

423rd Reserve Service Battalion. The battalion was organized in August 1918 at Camp Greene, North Carolina where it remained until it was demobilized in March 1919.

A view of the cantonment area at Camp Sheridan, Montgomery, Alabama. Courtesy Military History Institute.

Some of the colored troops stationed at Camp Johnston who are greatly appreciated by all because of their enter-taining qualities. Courtesy Military History Institute.

Labor Battalion entering pier ready to board the transport. Courtesy National Archives.

424th Reserve Service Battalion. The battalion was organized in August 1918 at Camp Governor's Island, New York where it remained until it was demobilized in May 1919.

425th Reserve Service Battalion. The battalion was organized in September 1918 at Fort Riley, Kansas where it remained until it was demobilized in April 1919.

426th Reserve Service Battalion. The battalion was organized in August 1918 at Camp Sevier, South Carolina where it remained until it was demobilized in March 1919.

427th Reserve Service Battalion. The battalion was organized in September 1918 at Camp Mills, New York it remained until it was demobilized in September 1919. (*See Chapter One – 316th Service Battalion*)

428th Reserve Service Battalion. The battalion was organized in August 1918 at Port Newark, New Jersey where it remained until it was demobilized at Camp Merritt, New Jersey March 1919.

429th Reserve Service Battalion. The battalion was organized in September 1918 at Camp Alexander, Virginia where it remained until it was demobilized in January 1919.

430th Reserve Service Battalion. The battalion was organized in September 1918 at Camp Alexander, Virginia where it remained until it was demobilized in March 1919.

431st Reserve Service Battalion. The battalion was organized in August 1918 at Camp Eustis, Virginia it was reassigned to Camp Upton, New York in January 1919 where it remained until it was demobilized in October 1919.

432nd Reserve Service Battalion. The battalion was organized in September 1918 at Camp Holabird, Maryland where it remained until it was demobilized in March 1919.

433rd Reserve Service Battalion. The battalion was organized in September 1918 at Camp Hancock, Georgia where it remained until it was demobilized in January 1919.

434th Reserve Service Battalion. The battalion was organized in October 1918 at Camp Logan, Texas where it remained until it was demobilized in March 1919.

435th Reserve Service Battalion. The battalion was organized in December 1918 at Camp Bowie, Texas where it remained until it was demobilized in May 1919.

436th Reserve Service Battalion. Never organized.

437th Reserve Service Battalion. The battalion was organized in September 1918 at Camp McClellan, Alabama where it remained until it was demobilized in March 1919.

438th Reserve Service Battalion. The battalion was organized in October 1918 at Camp Joseph E. Johnston, Florida where it remained until it was demobilized in January 1919.

439th Reserve Service Battalion. The battalion was organized in October 1918 at Camp Fort Sill, Oklahoma where it remained until it was demobilized in August 1919.

440th Reserve Service Battalion. Never organized.

441st Reserve Service Battalion. The battalion was organized in October 1918 at Camp Polk, North Carolina where it remained until it was demobilized in April 1919.

442nd Reserve Service Battalion. The battalion was organized in October 1918 at Camp Knox, Kentucky where it remained until it was demobilized in May 1919.

443rd Reserve Service Battalion. The battalion was organized in November 1918 at Camp Devens, Massachusetts where it remained until it was demobilized in May 1919.

444th Reserve Service Battalion. See Service Battalion 328th (Chapter One).

445th Reserve Service Battalion. The battalion was organized in October 1918 at Camp Stanley, Texas where it remained until it was demobilized in May 1919.

446th Reserve Service Battalion. The battalion was organized in October 1918 at Camp Mills, New York where it remained until it was demobilized in June 1919.

An unknown Black soldier poses for a studio portrait somewhere in the States. Courtesy Private Collection.

An unidentified Sergeant and wife pose for a portrait upon his return from France. Courtesy Private Collection.

Opposite: Private Harry McPhail sits for his Army photograph. Courtesy Private Collection.

447th Reserve Service Battalion. The battalion was organized in November 1918 at Camp A.A. Humphreys, Virginia where it remained until it was demobilized in April 1919.

448th Reserve Service Battalion. The battalion was organized in October 1918 at Camp Custer, Michigan where it remained until it was demobilized in July 1919.

449th Reserve Service Battalion. The battalion was organized in October 1918 at Camp Alexander, Virginia where it remained until it was demobilized in January 1919.

450th Reserve Service Battalion. Never organized.

Stevedore Regiments[10]

304th Stevedore Regiment. The regiment was activated at Camp Hill, Virginia in October 1917 and remained at Camp Hill as a training regiment. It was demobilized there in February 1918. The regiment consisted of regimental headquarters, headquarters and supply company, two battalions and a medical department with an aggregate strength of 2,498 (sixty-three white officers, 286 white enlisted men and 2,149 black enlisted men). The battalions consisted of a battalion headquarters and four companies. Each company consisted of four white officers and 250 black soldiers.[11]

Depot Brigades[12]

Depot Brigades held soldiers during the period of initial processing, training and indoctrination into the Army. They remained in these brigades until they were assigned to their operational unit. Black troops were assigned at selected Depot Brigades in all black companies. Following enactment of the Draft Law, there was much discussion about where black soldiers should be assigned as many whites, particularly Southern whites, worried that black soldiers might rise up against them if assigned in great numbers to a particular camp. This fear was reinforced after the August 1917 Houston Riot. In his book, The Trend of Races, George Haynes characterized the feeling as follows:

> "So aroused were some of the white people in some of the states about this matter, however, that officials and citizens presented many protests to the Government at Washington. The War Department first took that position that the Negro and white troops of the National Guard Divisions should be stationed at such posts as the exigencies of the service made necessary. After considerable conference, however, the Secretary of War modified the policy to the extent that while Southern states might take exception to the camps of Negro recruited for Northern states, they could not well object to the Negro draftee from the several districts of their own states. This worked hardships upon some of the draftees from states like Alabama, which had only a camp for the National Guardsmen. It did work out, however, that Negros from states like Georgia and Arkansas were thrown into cantonments with draftees from the North and West, and it soon developed that white and Negro men could get on together in the same camps without much friction."[13]

151st Depot Brigade. The brigade was formed at Camp Devens, Massachusetts in August 1917 it was demobilized at the same place in May 1919. Companies numbered 30, 51, 54, 55, 58 and 59 were formed with black soldiers.

152nd Depot Brigade. The brigade was formed at Camp Upton, New York in August 1917 it was demobilized at the same place in May 1919. Company 27 was formed with black soldiers.

153rd Depot Brigade. The brigade was formed at Camp Dix, New Jersey in August 1917 it was demobilized at the same place in May 1919. Companies numbered 52, 53, 56 were formed with black soldiers.

154th Depot Brigade. The brigade was formed at Camp Meade, Maryland in September 1917 it was demobilized at the same place in May 1919. Companies numbered 2, 16, 28, 38, 39 and 16th Company, 4th Development Battalion were formed with black soldiers.

155th Depot Brigade. The brigade was formed at Camp Lee, Virginia in September 1917 it was demobilized at the same place in May 1919. Companies numbered 39, 42, 44, 48, and 78 were formed with black soldiers.

156th Depot Brigade. The brigade was formed at Camp Jackson, South Carolina in September 1917 it was demobilized at the same place in May 1919. Companies 2 and 3 were formed with black soldiers. The 1st Provisional Regiment was a subordinate unit of the 156th Depot Brigade. It was formed in July 1918 at Camp Jackson, South Carolina it was demobilized November 1918 at Camp Sevier, South Carolina. Companies E, F &K 1st Provisional Regiment were composed of black soldiers.

157th Depot Brigade. The brigade was formed at Camp Gordon, Georgia in September 1917 it moved to Camp McClellan, Alabama in September 1918. It moved back to camp Gordon, Georgia in December 1918 and was demobilized at the same place in May 1919. Companies numbered 3, 11, 15, 41, 42, 43, 44, 45, 46, 47, 48, 49, 50, 51, 52, 58, 62, 75 in the 1st Provisional Regiment were formed with black soldiers.

158th Depot Brigade. The brigade was formed at Camp Sherman, Ohio in August 1917 it was demobilized at the same place in May 1919. Companies numbered 17, 28, 37, 39, 44, 48 were formed with black soldiers.

Opposite
Left: This unidentified Doughboy poses in a studio in front of a wonderful camp backdrop more representative of the nineteenth century. Courtesy Private Collection.

Right: An inductee at Camp Pike, Arkansas strikes a stern pose for the camera, this photo is back marked Ewing, Inc. Official Photographers, Division Exchange, Sixth Street, Opposite Depot, Camp Pike. Courtesy Private Collection.

Right: Two solders wearing Engineer collar insignia, pose in uniform somewhere in the States. Courtesy Private Collection.

159th Depot Brigade. The brigade was formed at Camp Zachary Taylor, Kentucky in August 1917 it was demobilized at the same place in May 1919. Companies numbered 44, 68 were formed with black soldiers.

160th Depot Brigade. The brigade was formed at Camp Custer, Michigan in September 1917 it was demobilized at the same place in May 1919. Companies numbered 11 and the 11th Provisional Regiment were formed with black soldiers.

161st Depot Brigade. The brigade was formed at Camp Grant, Illinois in August 1917 it was demobilized at the same place in May 1919. Companies numbered 48, 50, 51 were formed with black soldiers.

162nd Depot Brigade. The brigade was formed at Camp Pike, Arkansas in August 1917 it was demobilized at the same place in May 1919. Companies numbered 3,

Two buddies pose for a portrait in the States. Courtesy Private Collection.

7, 8, 10, 13, 14, 15, 17, 20, 28, 80, Companies G & M, 23rd Development Battalion were formed with black soldiers.

163rd Depot Brigade. The brigade was formed at Camp Dodge, Iowa in August1917 it was demobilized at the same place in May 1919. The 9th Battalion and companies numbered 2, 3, 65, G, Company, 1st Provisional Regiment, Company 4, 6th Provisional Regiment were formed with black soldiers.

164th Depot Brigade. The brigade was formed at Camp Funston, Kansas in September 1917 it was demobilized at the same place in May 1919. Company 5, 7th Provisional Regiment, were formed with black soldiers.

Provisional Battalions[14]

1st Provisional Regiment at Camp Jackson, South Carolina.
1st Provisional Regiment at Camp Grant, Illinois.
1st Provisional Depot Battalion, Camp Sevier, South Carolina.
1st Provisional Depot Brigade, Camp Sheridan, Alabama.

Development Battalions[15]

2nd and 3rd Development Battalion, Camp Upton, New York.
3rd and 4th Development Battalion, Camp Sherman, Ohio.
2nd Development Battalion, Camp Zachery Taylor, Kentucky.
3rd Development Battalion, Camp Custer, Michigan.
3rd Development Battalion, Camp Pike, Arkansas.
2nd Development Battalion, Camp Dodge, Iowa.
9th Development Battalion Main Training Group National Guard Troops, Camp Hancock,

This Baltimore, Maryland photograph of "Rob," an infantry soldier, shows a proud, bespeckled young man wearing the letters "U.S.A" and crossed rifles along with an unidentified patch on his overseas cap. Courtesy Private Collection.

Replacement Camps for Colored Troops[16]

Machine gun, Camp Hancock, Georgia.
Signal Corps, Fort Leavenworth, Kansas.
Ordnance, Hancock, Georgia.
Infantry, Camp Lee, Virginia.
Infantry, Camp Pike, Arkansas.
Field Artillery, Camp Jackson, South Carolina.
Quartermaster, Camp J.E. Johnston, Florida.

Miscellaneous Detachments[17]

Labor Detachment, Non-effective Company Number 3, Receiving Company Number 15, Camp J.E. Johnston, Florida.
Detention Camp, Camp McClellan, Alabama.
Detention Camp, Camp Shelby, Mississippi.
Headquarters Detachment, Camp Zachary Taylor, Kentucky.
Headquarters Detachment, Camp Travis, Texas.
Casual Detachment, Fort Riley, Kansas.
Casual Detachment, Camp Crane, Pennsylvania.
Casuals and Receiving Depot, Camp Pike, Arkansas.
1st Separate Battalion Adjutant General Department, Washington, D.C.
West Point Cavalry Detachment, West Point New York.
Army Service School Detachment, Fort Leavenworth, Kansas.
Mounted Service School Detachment, Fort Riley, Kansas.
Army War College Detachment, Washington Barracks, D.C.
Medical Corps Detachment, Camp Greenleaf, Georgia.
Base Hospital, Camp Meade, Maryland.
Base Hospital, Camp Zachary Taylor, Kentucky.
Dental unit, Camp Dix, New Jersey.
1st Sanitary Squad, Camp Hancock, Georgia.
Sanitary Corps Detachment, Camp J.E. Johnston, Florida.
Sanitary Corps Detachment, Camp Meade, Maryland.

Sanitary Corps Detachment, Camp Shelby, Mississippi.
Sanitary Corps Detachment, Camp Sevier, South Carolina.
Sanitary Corps Detachment, Camp Sheridan, Alabama.
Sanitary Corps Detachment, Camp Beauregard, Louisiana.
Sanitary Corps Detachment, Camp Eustis, Virginia.
Sanitary Corps Detachment, Camp Wheeler, Georgia.
Construction Companies Number 28 to 39 Langley Field, Virginia.
Quartermaster Detachment, Camp Cody, New Mexico.
Military police Detachment, Camp Travis, Texas.
Chemical Warfare Service, Edgewood, Maryland.

A group of four unknown soldiers pose back home before going overseas. Courtesy Private Collection.

Opposite
Left: A newly minted soldier stands guard in front of a stateside building with a Model 1917 Enfield rifle. Courtesy Private Collection.

Right: This soldier identified on the reverse as Croley was issued an outmoded Model 1902 tunic yet he carries the 1903 Springfield, the Army's newest rifle. Courtesy Private Collection.

This young unidentified soldier proudly sits in front of a United States Flag for his first military portrait. Courtesy Private Collection.

These two unidentified soldiers stand outside their barracks building with '03 Springfield rifles in hand. Courtesy Private Collection.

Left: A soldier stands in front of his barracks in the states. The back of the photo reads, "This is yours Mother. Mibis Marry Jemson – son. Goodbye to All." Courtesy Private Collection.

Opposite
Left: This soldier stands in a barren camp somewhere in the south, perhaps on the Border with Mexico. Courtesy Private Collection.

Right: This unidentified sergeant wears a mounted holster and stands in front of a studio backdrop to which an armored vehicle has been added.

Opposite
Left: Private George Cooper of Fife, Virginia poses for a portrait in the states wearing a prairie belt and civilian holster. The reverse of the photo reads, "Now in France." Courtesy Private Collection.

Right: This unknown soldier stands humbly in front of a studio backdrop of a tented camp. Courtesy Private Collection.

Above: Wearing Army Transport Corps insignia for this photo, this soldier may have well been a driver at one of the support detachments. Courtesy Private Collection.

Right: Home from Camp, this soldier stands in front of a civilian home. Courtesy Private Collection.

A regiment of black soldiers marches through town. Note the shoulder sleeve insignia indicating that this photo was taken after return from France. Also note the Red Cross banners hanging along the street. Courtesy Private Collection.

Opposite
Left: This unknown soldier strikes a pose standing in an overcoat with a United States flag as the backdrop. Courtesy Private Collection.

Right: A proud private first class stands on the porch of his home, just returned from the Army. Courtesy Private Collection.

This badly water damaged studio photo portrays a young infantry soldier and his lady just before he goes off to France. Courtesy Private Collection.

This touching photo of a soldier and his lady was taken before going overseas. Courtesy Private Collection.

Basic training to be a soldier – this young man stands at the ready with an M-1898 Kraig-Jorgensen rifle; a weapon considered obsolete by World War One, but used in great numbers for training in the States. Courtesy Private Collection.

Opposite: Two friends and newly minted soldiers pose with their new Army equipment in the States. Courtesy Private Collection.

Above: Two soldiers dressed as cooks pose with two soldiers in summer uniform at an Army Cantonment in the States. Courtesy Private Collection.

Opposite: Three friends pose in the States in their Army overcoats. Courtesy Private Collection.

Left: A compelling portrait of a young soldier wearing an Army Model 1909 drivers cap backward. Courtesy Private Collection.

Below: A truck full of black soldiers is loaded at a training camp; the reverse of the photo Post Card reads, "I got in the Camp all O.K. and will write later so good by I don't know if I pass." The Post Card was metered at the Camp Funston, Kansas Post Office on August 9, 1918 and is addressed to Miss Julia Hinderliter in Madison, Kansas. Many black units passed through Camp Funston. Courtesy Private Collection.

Opposite: This unusual photograph features a female friend of a soldier dressed in an Army uniform in front of what appears to be a barracks building. Courtesy Private Collection.

An unknown soldier poses in an Army overcoat after arriving back from France. Courtesy Private Collection.

This soldier poses in front of temporary building in a typical stateside training cantonment area. Courtesy Private Collection.

APPENDICES

Appendix 1
Listing of Colored Organizations of the Army

Divisions
92nd Division
Division Headquarters

183rd Infantry Brigade
365th Infantry Regiment
366th Infantry Regiment

184th Infantry Brigade
367th Infantry Regiment
368th Infantry Regiment
349th Machine Gun Battalion
350th Machine Gun Battalion
351st Machine Gun Battalion

167th Field Artillery Brigade
349th Field Artillery Regiment
350th Field Artillery Regiment
351st Field Artillery Regiment
317th Trench Mortar Battery
Headquarters Trains and Military Police
317th Sanitary Train
317th Supply Train
317th Ammunition Train
317th Engineer Train
317th Engineer Regiment
325th Field Signal Battalion
365th, 366th 367th 368th Ambulance Companies
365th, 366th 367th 368th Field Hospitals

93rd Division
369th Infantry Regiment
370th Infantry Regiment
371st Infantry Regiment
372nd Infantry Regiment

Engineer Service Battalions
505th through 567th Engineer Service Battalions

Regular Infantry
24th and 25th Infantry Regiments

Pioneer Infantry
6th Pioneer Infantry Regiment
60th through 65th Pioneer Infantry Regiments
801st through 817th Pioneer Infantry Regiments

Regular Cavalry Regiments
9th and 10th Cavalry Regiments

Quartermaster Corps
333rd and 383rd Bakery Company
322nd Butchery Company

Labor Battalions (Service Battalions)
301st through 350th Labor Battalions
401st through 450th Labor Battalions
316th Laundry Company

Motor Transport Corps
22nd and 598th Motor Truck Company

Transportation Corps
801st through 868th Stevedore Companies

Depot Brigades
151st through 164th (selected companies contained black soldiers in these brigades)

Development Battalions
Battalions at Camp Upton, New York, Camp Sherman, Ohio, Camp Zachery Taylor, Kentucky, Camp Custer, Michigan, Camp Pike, Arkansas, Camp Hancock, Georgia, and Camp Dodge, Iowa.

Replacement Camps
Machine Gun, Camp Hancock, Georgia, Signal Corps, Fort Leavenworth, Kansas, Ordnance, Camp Hancock, Georgia, Infantry, Camp Lee, Virginia and Camp Pike, Arkansas, Field Artillery, Camp Jackson, South Carolina, and Quartermaster, camp Joseph E. Johnston, Florida.

Miscellaneous Detachments
Labor Detachment Non-Effective Company Number 3, and Receiving Company 15, Camp Joseph E. Johnston, Florida, Detention Camp, Camp Mc-Clellan, Alabama, Detention Camp, Camp Shelby, Mississippi, Headquarters Detachment, Camp Zachery Taylor, Kentucky, Headquarters Detachment, Camp Travis, Texas, Casual Detachment, Fort Riley, Kansas, Casual Detachment, Camp Crane, Pennsylvania, Casuals and Receiving Depot, Camp Pike, Arkansas, Infantry, attached to Depot Brigade at Camp Dix, New Jersey and Camp Custer, Michigan, 1st Separate Battalion, Adjutant General's Department, Washington, D.C., West Point Cavalry Detachment, West Point, New York, Army Service School Detachment, Fort Leavenworth, Kansas, Army War College Detachment, Washington Barracks, Washington, D.C., Medical Corps, Camp Greenleaf, Georgia, Base Hospital Camp Meade, Maryland and Camp Zachery Taylor, Kentucky, Dental Unit, Fort Dix, New Jersey, 1st Sanitary Squad, Camp Hancock, Georgia, Sanitary Corps Detachments at Camp Joseph E. Johnson, Florida, Camp Meade, Maryland, Camp Shelby, Mississippi, Camp Sevier, South Carolina, Camp Sheridan, Alabama, Camp Beauregard, Louisiana, Camp Eustis, Virginia, and Camp Wheeler, Georgia, Construction

Companies Number 28 to 39, Langley Field, Virginia, Quarermaster Detachment, Camp Cody, New Mexico, Military Police Detachment, Camp Travis, Texas, Chemical Warfare Service, Edgewood, Maryland.

Student Army training Corps Detachments
Institute West Virginia, Tuskegee Institute, Western University, Quindaro, Kansas, Prairie View Normal, Prairie, Texas, Branch Normal School, Pine Bluff, Arkansas, Hampton Institute, Hampton, Virginia, Shaw University, Raleigh, North Carolina, Negro Agricultural and Technical College, Greensboro, North Carolina, Atlanta University, Atlanta, Georgia, Wilberforce University, Xenia,

Ohio, South Carolina Agricultural and Mechanical College, Orangeburg, South Carolina, Fiske University, Nashville, Tennessee, Howard university, Washington, D.C.

Note: Information gathered from Rolls and Rosters Section of the Adjutant Generals Office, the Returns Section of the Adjutant General Office and the Organizational Directory of the United States Army, 1919, also War Department Historical Section Correspondence File Number 2957 all from the collections of Military History Institute, Carlisle, Pennsylvania.

Authors' Note: As mentioned in the foreword, we have included the heretofore unpublished War College study on the recommended future use of "Negro Manpower." We felt that this study, published shortly after the war, illuminated the significant obstacles that black soldiers had yet to overcome. Sadly, the heroic deeds of the brave black soldiers of World War I would fall victim to the narrow views and prevailing racial prejudice of the period. The study that follows served as the starting point for Army assignment practices at the beginning of World War II. It would not be until President Truman's Executive Order of 1948, directing integration of the Army, that black soldiers would finally be allowed to serve alongside of whites.

Appendix 2
Notes on proposal plan for use of Negro manpower.
August 3, 1926.
(Not a part of the plan.)

1. The fundamental conception upon which this plan is based is that the military man power of the United States, white or black, should be assigned to duties in the Army for which it is qualified. Military considerations alone should govern in war.
2. The negro does not perform his share of civil duties in time of peace in proportion to his population. He has no leaders in industrial or commercial life. He takes no part in government. Compared to the white man he is admittedly of inferior mentality. He is inherently weak in character.
3. The negro issue should be met squarely. The War Department had no predetermined and sound plan for the use of negro troops at the beginning of the World War. It had no adequate defense against political and racial pressure and was forced to organize negro combat divisions and commission unqualified negro officers. The results are well known.
4. The War Department when occasion demands should be able to present this matter frankly to those who make demands or should know the facts.
   The negro, particularly the officer, failed in the World War.
   The door will not be closed against him on this account.
   He will be given an opportunity to take part in war in accordance with his qualifications in exactly the same fields of activity as are allotted the white man.
   He will be accepted for service by the identical standards applied to the white man.
   While in the service he will be measured by the standards applied to the white man. This includes reclassification, elimination, and rewards of promotion and decoration.
   He will be given a sound plan of organization, training and leadership.
   He will be given tasks he may reasonably be expected to
   perform.
   If he makes good he will have the opportunity eventually to fight in the war with all-negro organizations.
   If he fails to qualify to fight as a race he will be limited to such tasks as he can perform under white leadership.
   What he accomplishes in war will depend upon the negro.
5. There should be no sentiment about the use of negro troops in war.
   It is not sound to contend that he should bear losses
   in war in proportion to his population relative to white population. The basis of his employment in war should be that applied to white soldiers, via., qualifications and capabilities for military service.
   In the American Expeditionary Forces in France the negro's total share of losses was 1-1/2%.
6. If the negro should be called into service on a plan based on the numerical strength of his population his share of man power for the Mobilization Plan

would be almost twice the quota, which under the standards developed in the World War, he can furnish.
7. The Mobilization Plan provides for approximately 140,000 negroes for non-combatant duty. This would leave approximately 30,000 for the experiment of combat duty.
8. The majority of negroes left at home will be in the southern states where they will be needed for labor and where they can best be handled by competent whites.

THE ARMY WAR COLLEGE
OFFICE OF THE COMMANDANT

Washington Barracks, D.C.
October 30, 1925.

MEMORANDUM FOR THE CHIEF OF STAFF:

Subject: The use of negro man power in war.

I. Papers accompanying.
Reference "A". Analysis of the physical, mental, moral and psychological qualities and characteristics of the negro as a sub-species of the human family.
Reference "B". Performance of the negro in past wars.
Reference "C". The negro officer.
Reference "D". Negro political activity in the World War.
Reference "E". Plan for the organization and employment in war of the negro man power drafted and found physically and mentally qualified for military service.

II. The problem presented.
Under the Constitution the negro has the rights of citizenship. He forms a considerable part of the population of the United States. It is evident that he must bear his share of the burden of war.
To what extent shall negro man power be used in a military effort contemplated by the War Department General Mobilization Plan?
How shall it be organized?
How shall it be officered?
How shall it be trained and employed in the Theatre of Operations and the Zone of the Interior?
What standards should be used in the appointment and promotion of negro officers?

III. Facts bearing upon the problem.
1. The negro is physically qualified for combat duty.
He is by nature subservient and believes himself to be inferior to the white man.
He is most susceptible to the influence of crowd psychology.
He can not control himself in the face of danger to the extent the white man can.
He had not the initiative and resourcefulness of the white man.
He is mentally inferior to the white man. Reference "A".
2. In past wars the negro has made a fair laborer.
As a technician and a fighter he has been inferior to the white man. Reference "B".
3. In the World War the negro officer was a failure in combat. Reference "C".
4. In the World War political pressure forced the formation of two negro combat divisions and the commissioning of about 600 negro officers. Reference "D".

5. There are 11,000,000 negroes in the United States. The total number which according to the standards developed in the World War are qualified to be soldiers is 352,922. Applying the same standards to the white man we find that the negro can furnish 6.1% of the total man power in the United States qualified for military service. On this basis his contribution of man power to the total required by the War Department General Mobilization Plan is 209,679. Reference "E".

IV. <u>Opinion of the War College.</u>

1. In the process of evolution the American negro has not progressed as far as the other sub-species of the human family. As a race he has not developed leadership qualities. His mental inferiority and the inherent weakness of his character are factors that must be considered with great care in the preparation of any plan for his employment in war.

2. The life of the nation is at stake in war. Neither the white man nor the negro should be given tasks they are not qualified to perform. However, the plan for the use of the man power of the United States in war should be fair to both races.

3. In past wars the negro has made a fair laborer, but an inferior technician. As a fighter he has been inferior to the white man even when led by white officers.

4. The negro officer was a failure as a combat officer in the World War.

5. The door should not be closed against the negro because of his failure in the World War. He should be given a fair opportunity to perform the tasks in war for which he is qualified or may qualify himself under a sound plan of organization, training and leadership. He should be measured by the same standards applied to the white man. Finally, he should be given an opportunity to demonstrate as a race his competency for combat duty.

6. In making effective the War Department General Mobilization Plan the total number of negroes to be taken into the military service should be 209,679.

7. The largest negro unit that should be organized on mobilization is the battalion. These battalions should be assigned to divisions of the Regular Army and the National Guard in the proportion of one battalion to a division in combat training. If and when these battalions demonstrate satisfactory combat efficiency they should be grouped progressively into larger units with the division as the ultimate aim.

8. Negro soldiers as individuals should not be assigned to white units.

9. The total number of negro combat units to be organized on mobilization should be sufficient to form one complete Infantry division less headquarters of larger units. This number should be organized into battalions, trains, etc., and distributed by services and branches in the proportions indicated by tables of organization for the Infantry division. The remainder of the negro quota, after deducting the number necessary for training and replacement purposes and frontier and other duty in the Zone of the Interior, should be assigned to the Engineers, Quartermaster Corps, Air Service, Cavalry, Coast Artillery, and Medical Department in accordance with the occupational qualifications of the men and the needs of these services.

10. At the beginning of the war the negro combat units should be officered entirely by white officers except in the grade of lieutenant. Only negro officers who hereafter graduate from training camps where they have qualified for appointment as combat officers in accordance with standards applied to white candidates should be assigned to these units. The white officers assigned to negro combat units should be carefully selected.

11. White and negro lieutenants should be assigned to negro combat units in numbers to insure that at all times the companies will have double the number of lieutenants in corresponding white organizations. During the period of combat training the number of negro lieutenants in negro combat units should not exceed the number of white lieutenants.

12. Initially negro officers above the grade of lieutenant, and all other negro officers not included in Par. 10 above, should be assigned in general to non-combatant units of negro troops. They should be observed, tested, reclassified, eliminated or advanced eventually to combat assignments in accordance with the standards applied to white officers.

13. Negro officers should not be placed over white officers, noncommissioned officers or soldiers.

14. Negro officer candidates should attend training camps with white candidates. They should have the same instructors, take the same test and meet the same requirements for appointment as officers as the white candidates. They should be sheltered, messed and instructed separately from white candidates.

15. Citations, decorations, and promotion for demonstrated efficiency should be given the negro in accordance with the standards applied to the white man.

16. This plan provides for the initial assignment of negro man power at the outbreak of war. It will be seen that the eventual use of the negro will be determined by his performances in combat training and service. If and when the battalions assigned to white divisions qualify for combat service they will be assigned to this duty. If the negro makes good the way is left open for him to go into combat eventually with all-negro units. If the negro officer fails to demonstrate his ability to lead his own troops they will be led by white officers. The formation of <u>all-negro</u> units should be made gradually, starting with the company. They should be led by negro officers who have demonstrated their ability to lead. When they have qualified for combat duty they should be given an opportunity to demonstrate in combat whether or not they should progress to larger units.

17. This guiding principle in this plan is military efficiency.

The plan is believed to be eminently fair to both the negro and the white man.

Political or racial pressure should not be allowed to alter it.

V. <u>Action recommended.</u>

It is recommended that this study be taken as the basis of the policy of the War Department for the use of negro man power and that the plans proposed herein be used as a guide in the revision of the War Department General Mobilization Plan.

IV. <u>Concurrences.</u>

The policies and plan for the use of negro man power proposed in this study are the culmination of several years study by the faculty and student body of The Army War College.

M.E. ELI, Major General, U.S. Army, Commandant.

REFERENCE "A".
ANALYSIS OF PHYSICAL, MENTAL, MORAL, AND PSYCHOLOGICAL QUALITIES AND CHARACTERISTICS OF THE NEGRO

1. <u>Physical.</u>

During the World War statistics indicate that rejection of Class I registrants for white and negro races were, respectively, 30.29% and 25.40%. Without investigation this might seem to indicate that the negro is physically superior to the white. It appears, however, that the standards prescribed for the white were not maintained for the negro. Rates of non-effectives in negro units were so high as to cause a protest from General Pershing. He wired, "Colored Stevedore troops arriving with tuberculosis, old fractures, extreme flat feet, hernia, venereal diseases all existing prior to enlistment, not able to stand hardship of climate and travel, larger proportion of sick than among white troops. Recommend elimination of unfit by rigid physical examination before embarking."

"Based upon his observation of the poor physical condition of colored stevedore troops, orders were issued to eliminate the physical unfit negroes before their departure from a port of embarkation. After the issue of such orders, 43% of 3,604 colored drafted men from Camp Pike to Newport News were found unfit for overseas carriers on medical examination at the port of embarkation. Authority had, however, been given in this case to send on from Camp Pike men suffering from venereal diseases but not receiving daily treatment."

"The physical condition of a large part of the colored draft is very poor. Many must be entirely eliminated and a large proportion of these left are not fit for combat duty." – Lytle Brown, Assistant Chief of Staff, War Plans Division to Chief of Staff.

"A further examination into this case shows that the Commanding General, Camp Pike, was not trying to unload undesirables on the Port of Embarkation. He realized they were not fit for overseas service and he sent the pick of what he had but that is the class of man the colored drafted men were. Other examples could be given but it would be cumulative testimony along the same lines." – Col. E.D. Anderson, General Staff, Chairman, Operations Branch.

Taking this case, which is stated to be more or less typical, the Surgeon at Camp Pike stated: "From a conservative estimate I will state that fully 90% of all negroes received at the Depot Brigade, now have or have and venereal disease in some form."

The situation with reference to the physical condition of negroes during the war is shown in the following quotation from a report from Col. Anderson to the Chief of Staff: - "The present policy is to accept men with certain ailments along this line and to send them to the camps to receive the necessary treatment before starting them on their training. The large percentage of colored men temporarily unfit reduces the effective strength while the space they occupy might well be used by able bodied men." This difference between whites and negroes is also apparent in the disability discharge rate which was, respectively, 42 and 80 per thousand.

From this it is clear that the number of physical defectives among the negroes was much higher than among the whites and that full weight can not be given to the figures of the Provost Marshal General, as different standards were used in the physical examinations of white and negro draftees. It can be further deduced from this that the negro is physically inferior to the white man and that more rigid examinations must be conducted in the next war. The Southern negroes, who form the bulk of the race - their endurance and stamina in cold rigorous climates is low. His normal physical activity is generally small due to his laziness.

2. Mental.

It is generally recognized that the pure blood American negro is inferior to our white population in useful capacity. Such negroes as have shown marked mental attainments also show a heavy strain of white blood.

"The negroes are descended from slaves imported from West Africa. Their characteristics, physically, were formerly quite uniform and show them to be very low in the scale of human evolution." The cranial cavity of the negro is smaller than the white; his brain weighing 35 ounces contrasted with the 45 for the white.

The intelligence of the negro is shown in his inability to compete with the white in professions and other activities in peace time when mental equipment is an essential for success.

To turn to a statistical proof of this mental inferiority we have only to consider the intelligence test conducted during the war.

All officers, without exception, agree that the negro lacks initiative, displays little or no leadership, and cannot accept responsibility. Some point out that these defects are greater in the Southern negro.

3. Morale.

As judged by white standards, the negro is unmoral. His ideas with relation to humor and sex relations are not on the same plane as those of our white population. Petty thieving, lying, and promiscuity are much more common among negroes than among whites. Activities connected with white women have been the cause of considerable trouble among negroes. Experience before and in the World War showed that the negro will protect his color in cases of emergency without regard to truth. The same lack of honesty was evident with reference to reports, the lack of information being supplied from an active imagination.

"The negro officer has in my opinion been a failure. He has not the fine points of honor which should characterize the American Army officer." – Commanding Officer of Regt. Of 92nd Division.

"I do not remember of a single patrol report coming from an officer that ever gave sufficient information and practically every report had to be checked by some white officer. The check nearly always showed total ignorance on the part of the negro leader and usually a disregard of truth. Also, it is another fact which we found that colored officers cliqued together and sought at all times to protect the members of their own race, no matter whether they were right or wrong." – Chief of Staff, 92nd Division.

"The conclusion forced by the observation of a large number of cases was that the colored officer was of almost no value in the conduct of night patrols. He would perhaps go out a short distance, kill a lot of time, and return with a report of conditions as could just as readily have been written if he had not gone out at all. Or, by some flight of the imagination, he would concoct a fanciful story of places and events entirely non-existent, but difficult to disprove at the time." – Commanding Officer, 92nd Division.

If this was the state of affairs among their more intelligent picked men, i.e., their officers, the situation with regard to the rank and file can be well imagined.

4. Psychological.

One is inclined to believe that a member of one race is not fitted to write authoritatively on the psychology of another. The white mind and the negro mind are very different. Some people claim to understand the negroes while others whose opinions are of just as much weight say that this is impossible. There are, however, certain factors that influence the psychology of the American negro and to a certain extent we may go.

All American negroes are descendents of some tribe or tribes of Africa. From these antecedents the negro inherits a profoundly superstitious nature. The belief in fetishes exists to this day and the negro will still take great stock in signs and omens. These are very real to the negro and overpower and at times supplant the veneer of religious culture he has acquired from the whites.

The negroes racial experience as a slave has bred in him a peculiar form of mind. He has become by nature sub-servient. He instinctively regards the white man as his superior. He is willing to give way to the white man as a general rule and he does this unthinkingly. His period of service as a slave and his mental caliber cause him to accept unhesitatingly as proper and natural, work that would disgust the white.

In general the negro is jelly, docile and tractable, and lively but with harsh or unkind treatment can become stubborn, sullen and unruly. Innate secretiveness is a part of his nature. This may be a result of his period of existence as a slave. It was then his one sure weapon of defense, as a race, against the whites.

A curious feature of the negro's psychology is his susceptibility to the influence of crowd psychology. We have had some painful experiences along this line in the army, notably the Brownsville riot. Other cases have occurred entirely without the military establishment wherein crowd psychology has seized upon a mass or group of negroes and precipitated a race war. It is useless to examine the causes of these for the plain facts are that regardless of causes individual negroes of the crowd would never have behaved as they have done were it not for the influence of the crowd. There is no race that is not susceptible to crowd psychology but the negro is easier swayed by it and harder to control when under its influence than others.

Closely allied to crowd psychology is the question of physical courage. In physical courage it must be admitted that the American negro falls well back of the white man and possibly behind all other races. All men, if not actually afraid of death are anxious in varying measures to avoid it. Self-preservation is said to be the first law of nature and self-preservation is but the natural avoidance of an early extinction. All members of the human family in common with all animals possess the instinct for self-preservation and the negro probably possesses it in no greater measure than the rest of mankind. The white, in general, is able to control his fear in the presence of danger and keep about the occupation in which he is engaged with at least a semblance of coolness. The negro, on the other hand, is not so capable in controlling the instinct of self-preservation. His psychological makeup is such that he unable to control his emotions beyond a certain point. When this point is reached the "cave in" occurs and then all of his efforts are bent on self-preservation. Duty, propriety, discretion and obligation are all thrown to the winds. This cannot, however, be held against him. No reasoning being can expect more of a certain nature than exists in that nature. The reason that the negro gives way under fear of some danger is exactly the same reason as that which causes the white to do the same, only the negro is likely to do so under less pressure than the white and consequently his breaking point will come more quickly. It may be likened to putting a continually increasing strain on a rope. It finally breaks because the material of which it is made is not strong enough to stand the added pull. There is this to be said however: As the negro recognizes the white as his superior he will under white control, and in the presence of whites, stand much greater pressure from impending danger than he will in a group of negroes alone. Another feature that affects the psychology of the negro is his close association with the white race during the past two centuries. This has had an effect in two ways. Within limits the negro has acquired a veneer of the white man's culture. The negro has taken up the white man's religion and while with some the matter of religious conviction is deep-seated and real in general, it is believed to be superficial; and, were contact with the whites removed, would soon degenerate into superstitious forms or be effaced entirely. No race could have stood the amount of oppressions in the form of slavery, openly expressed contempt, injustice, enforced segregation, etc., that the negro has from the white without evolving a form of psychology against the white. It would be futile for us to try to believe that the negro has no peculiar state of mind against us. He undoubtedly has. While the negro must feel some tinge of resentment against the race that has enslaved him in the past and now holds him as a thing apart, it must be agreed that this state of mind is to a great extent allayed by the innate easy-going nature of the negro.

The psychology of the negro on heredity derived from his mediocre African ancestors, cultivated by several generations of slavery, followed by about three generations of evolution from slavery in the anomalous state of legal without actual equality with the white, is one from which we cannot expect to draw leadership material.

Summarizing these characteristics, it appears that:

The negro is profoundly superstitious.

He is by nature sub-servient and naturally believes himself inferior to the white.

He is jolly, tractable, lively and docile by nature, but through real or supposed harsh or unjust treatment may become sullen and stubborn.

He is very susceptible to the influence of crowd psychology. In consequence of this a panic among negro troops is much more serious and harder to control than one among whites.

The psychology of the negro is such that we may not expect to draw leadership material from his race. The negro has not a great deal of confidence in leaders of this own race and it would be an impossibility to place leaders of his race over whites.

The psychology of the negro is such that with whites as leaders he can serve in combat troops. He has confidence in the superiority of the white and the fact that whites are with him in time of danger puts off the time when his courage gives out.

He has not the physical courage of the white. He simply cannot control himself in fear of some danger in the degree that the white can.

His psychology is such that he willing accepts hard labor and for this reason can well be employed in labor troops or other non-combatant branches.

The negro is unmoral. He simply does not see that certain things are wrong.

The negro race is one of the most secretive in the world.

While the negro undoubtedly has a state of mind bordering on resentment directed against the white, this feeling is numbed by his easy-going nature.

The negro's growing sense of importance will make them more and more of a problem, and racial troubles may be expected to increase.

5. Social.

The negro's physical, mental, moral, and other psychological characteristics have made it impossible for him to associate socially with any except the lowest class of whites. The only exceptions to this are the negro concubines who have sometimes attracted men who, except for this association, were considered high class.

This social inequality makes the close association of whites and blacks in military organization inimicable to harmony and efficiency.

REFERENCE "B"
PERFORMANCE OF NEGRO IN PAST WARS.

I. Introduction.
The performance of the negro in past wars deals solely with the American negros. It must be remembered that French colored troops are exclusively recruited from among the most mentally primitive populations and it would be impossible to compare them to the colored population of the United States. Even the French dark skinned Colonel levies in the World War have been found available as combat troops only in very limited numbers and under special conditions and long and slow training by competent officers.

II. Period prior to the World War.
1. During the Revolutionary War few negroes were used, but not one unit composed entirely of negroes was ever raised. The so called "Rhode Island Black Regiment" was a battalion of four companies organized in 1778; less than half were negroes and their service was apparently satisfactory.
2. Two battalions of negroes participated in the Battle of New Orleans (War of 1812), where they fought behind entrenchments with white troops, closely supported by artillery. All the officers were white and their service was apparently satisfactory.
3. In the Civil War after the Emancipation Proclamation (Jan. 1, 1863) some 178,000 negroes were mustered into the service, as infantry, cavalry and artillery. With but few exceptions their officers were white. Their service met with many commendatory orders, but instances arose where units were reported incompetent, and cases of mutinies and misbehavior also occurred when leadership was not efficient.
4. During the Indian Campaigns, Spanish War and Philippines Insurrection the Regular negro regiments participated in a number of engagements. Their officers were almost without exception white and the noncommissioned officers and many men had long service, and were well disciplined. Their service was satisfactory.
5. Prior to the World War several instances have occurred of note between negro soldiers and white civilians, such as the Houston and Brownsville affairs.

III. World War Record of the Negro.
1. During the World War great numbers of labor and service battalions were raised from the negroes. A complete combat division, the 92nd, was organized in which the company officers of infantry and machine gun units were negroes. This division had service on the quiet fronts and in reserve in the Argonne, one regiment of which was in the front line. Its conduct was so bad that it was removed in a few days, the regimental commander asking for the removal of 35 negro officers for inefficiency and cowardice. The organizations that had white officers were markedly superior in this division to those that had colored. The trains and special services were reasonably efficient. The heavy artillery regiment with all white officers was the best negro unit.
2. The 93rd Division really consisted of four separate infantry regiments and served under the French. In one regiment all officers were white, in two others where there had been colored officers, whites finally replaced them. In the third a regular white officer commanded. These units did good service but were not up to the standards of either our own or French white organizations.

IV. The Negro in Labor Units.
1. The negro has run true to form as regards his occupational classifications. He is exceptionally well fitted for Pioneer Infantry, Supply Trains (Animal or Motor Drawn), Labor Troops S.O.S., Remount Depots, Home Guards at Supply Depots, Service Detachments at Corps, Army and S.O.S., Headquarters, and at the many schools in constant operation. Experience has shown that cooks and waiters at officers' messes in all except divisional or corps troops, might well be colored. Thousands of men are needed on lines of communication and for ground work with the air services. Service such as is performed by the Colored Detachment at West Point might well be performed by colored soldiers at all headquarters from Division up.
2. An opinion expressed by many experienced officers who have had long service with negro troops is as follows:
"The negro does not desire combat duty under conditions of present day warfare. That if when drafted into service he was given a choice of assignment to a combat organization or to a "Labor Battalion" (a more attractive title would be better for this class of duty, e.g., 'Service of Conservation and Repair') the majority would choose the less dangerous service."

V. Combat Characteristics of the Negro.
1. Generally speaking, taking the average of the Draft, only about six percent – less than – percent – have the characteristics to be combat soldiers – from the mental standpoint alone, hence the difficulty of finding suitable noncommissioned officers, for they must not only be mentally fit, but likewise possess initiative and courage.
2. An opinion held in common by practically all officers is that the negro is a rank coward in the dark. His fear of the unknown and unseen will prevent him from ever operating as an individual scout with success. His lack of veracity causes unsatisfactory reports to be rendered, particularly on patrol duty.
3. World War experience implies that the negro may not stand grilling combat with heavy losses. In general the negro has confidence in white leaders and granted proper initial training before going into battle, he will follow the white leader with the utmost bravery. One of the peculiarities of the negro as a soldier is that he has no confidence in his negro leaders, nor will he follow a negro officer into battle, no matter how good the officer may be, with the same confidence and lack of fear that he will follow a white man. This last trait has been so universally reported by all commanders that it cannot be considered as a theory – the negroes themselves recognize it as a fact.

VI. Combat training for the Negro.
1. The negro needs trained leadership far more than the white man needs it, and above all they need leaders in whom they have confidence, and whose presence they can feel and see at all times.
2. On account of the inherent weaknesses in negro character, especially general lack of intelligence and initiative, it requires much longer time of preliminary training to bring a negro organization up to the point of training where it is fit for combat, than it does in the case of white men. All theoretical instruction is beyond the mental grasp of the negro – it must be intensely practical, supplemented by plain talks explaining the reasons for things in simple terms. It is necessary to distinguish the negroes' ability to summarize a subject from a true understanding of this subject. Since a large amount of individual instruction will be found necessary in a negro organization, it is desirable to have about double the number of instructors with them as with a white organization. Due to the special necessity of close observation in the lower units of negro organizations – platoons – the same need of a double complement of lieutenants in combat is apparent.
3. On account of the ever present danger of "rape cases" and the conflict between the economic side of the question and racial feeling, the negro, generally speaking, should be trained in the locality from which drafted, and there should never be a time when the negro organizations are not very much in the minority in any camp (general opinion is that they should never exceed 1/3 the strength of any camp).

VII. Size of Negro Combat Units.
1. Due to his susceptibility to "Crowd Psychology" a large mass of negroes, e.g., a division, is very subject to panic. Experience has indicated that the negroes produce better results by segregation and cause less trouble. Grouping of negroes generally in the past has produced demands for equality, both during war and after demobilization. The 92nd Division was a failure, admitted by all competent officers in the division and by other trained observers and leaders.

Many of our Organized Reserve Divisions are approaching completion as to units. Their organization in voluntary – to force a negro unit upon them would mean their disintegration as soon as the present obligation of the officers expired.
2. General Pershing stated that he wanted organizations no larger than a regiment to be used as were the regiments of the 93rd Division. The defeat of a regiment would stop the action of a division and possibly that of a corps, it can hardly cause disaster to an army, nor, if reserves are available, to a corps or division. A regiment in defense generally has 2 battalions on the line – the negro is weak on defense and especially liable to losses in raids. The best opinion on the subject is a compromise between safety and morals in choosing between a regiment and a battalion would favor the selection of the battalion as the largest negro unit initially.

3. There is no apparent reason why one arm of the service should use negro troops and another should not. One arm may require more educated men and specialists than another, but so long as men of suitable qualifications can be found, there is no reason to exempt the arm. On the other hand it would be foolish to make up any arm of men lacking the necessary qualifications.

VIII. Detailed Extracts from various sources relative to the performance of Negro in Past Wars.

1. All of the foregoing data is a general statement arranged in narrative form but extracts from signed, official statements of competent military officers who had the interests of the negro at heart, but not to the exclusion of making any lowering of the required standards for military efficiency in battle. The general trend of these comments may be summed up as follows:

"The services of the negro in past wars has been most satisfactory in the capacity of labor troops and while not entirely satisfactory in combat, he should be given an opportunity to prove his worth under trained leaders, preferably white."

2. The following extract are given in complete detail: (a) Extract from Supplement No. 1 to Report of Committee No. 7 entitled "Historical Study of the Employment of Negro Manpower in war".

UNITED STATES.
Introduction.
So far as the United States is concerned we may consider the negro to be descended from the slaves who were imported principally during the Eighteenth and early part of the Nineteenth Century from the West Coast of Africa. They belonged to the true negro stock, which shows great similarity of physical characteristics, qualities which have been greatly altered due to continued crossing with whites since arrival in this country.

The West Coast negro, according to the best authorities, is very low in the scale of human elevation; his brain capacity averages about 35 ounces as contrasted with the white men's 45 ounces. He did not belong to the warrior tribes, such as are found in South Africa, but on the contrary was peaceable, indolent and backward.

After being brought to this country his status as a slave gave him almost no legal rights, did little to raise his moral standards, and instead of producing the qualities so necessary in a soldier of individual courage, initiative and pride of nationality or race, acted in quite the contrary manner. These facts are necessary to consider in studying the history of the American negro in the various wars in which he has participated.

The study herewith is merely an outline with such conclusions as seemed pertinent.

Revolutionary War.
The question of employing negroes as soldiers was considered very early in the Revolution. In 1775 Washington prohibited in orders the enlistment of any negro. Notwithstanding this fact, it seems evident that a few free negroes had been in the army since the beginning of the war. Later the reenlistment of much of these as had been discharged was authorized.

A number of efforts were made during the course of the war by various individuals to get the States to enlist slaves, the reward being freedom. Most of these plans were not favorably received. However, there is no doubt that during the entire war, negro slaves and freedom were in the ranks and continued to be enlisted in most of the States, especially when the pressure for recruits increased toward the latter years of the struggle. A return of August, 1779, showed 755 in Washington's Army two months after the Battle of Monmouth.

An attempt to raise a negro organization was made in one instance only: this was the so-called "Rhode Island Black Regiment", authorized by the legislature of that State in 1778. It really was a battalion of four companies, and participated creditably in a number of actions from 1778 until the end of the war. The greatest number of negroes in the organization was in 1780, at which time 150 of its enlisted personnel were negroes, all of the officers being white. Many references are made of this being a negro organization, which is contrary to the facts shown above, for at no time was half of its strength colored.

Conclusion.
Apparently the principal reason for the enlistment of negroes was the difficulty of obtaining other recruits. No unit composed entirely of negroes was raised, and only in the Rhode Island Black Regiment was there an appreciable number. Here they were combat soldiers; elsewhere no reference has been found of the character of their employment. In this mixed organization they apparently performed satisfactory service.

The War of 1812.
During the earlier part of the war no colored troops were used, but as the struggle continued recruits became scarce as during the Revolution and again some steps were taken to enlist negroes. In October 1814, the Legislature of New York authorized the raising of two colored regiments, but no record has been found that indicates they were actually mustered into the service. However, some individuals were enlisted.

In September 1814, Andrew Johnson authorized the formation of two battalions of negro freeman which were commanded by Colonel Lacoste and Major D'Aquin. Both of these units had white officers and were on the line at the battle of New Orleans. No specific record of their performance is given by Lossing other than the fact that the points where they were located which were in the vicinity of the American batteries, were not penetrated by the British attack, and apparently they performed their duty without criticism.

Conclusion.
Behind entrenchments, under white officers and with white troops on both sides and on the defensive, the negro troops behaved properly and gave satisfactory service.

The Mexican War.
No record has been found of the use of any negro troops during this period, and it is most probable that no separate colored units were formed.

The Civil War.
(a) The Union Army.
Prior to 1863 no use was made of negro troops by the Northern States; a number of plans had been discussed, but no action taken until President Lincoln's Emancipation Proclamation was issued on January 1st, 1863, which among other provisions, declared that negroes would be admitted into the armed forces. The policy was to have white officers, although a few negroes were commissioned. During the war some 178,000 colored troops were enlisted which were organized into: five regiments of engineers, later turned into infantry; thirteen regiments of heavy artillery, one regiment and one battery of light artillery; one hundred and thirty-eight regiments and three companies of infantry. In several instances these regiments were grouped into and operated as divisions.

It is exceedingly difficult to get accurate information as to the negro troops in this war. To call out the facts from the records of the Rebellion would be a task entirely out of question in the time we are allotted for this study, and most writers on the subject have been either negroes or persons who approached the subject from a sentimental standpoint, both having as motives the glorification of the negro.

Negro troops actually took part in many of the battles of the latter part of the war among them Port Hudson, Fort Wagner, Fort Pillow, Petersburg, Nashville and Fort Fisher. Their conduct as a whole was good. However, there were instances of incompetence and even of mutiny as at Port Hudson where an entire regiment participated in a riot, attempting to shoot one of the officers. A number of the ringleaders were sentenced to be shot for this affair.

(b) The Confederate Army.
From the earliest days of the war negroes had been used by the Confederacy for work on fortifications and as teamsters and cooks. However, no steps were taken to regularly organize them as soldiers until late in the fall of 1864, when the Confederate Congress passed a law authorizing their use, but by not giving freedom to the slaves enlisted practically nullified the effect of the legislation. While a few negro companies were raised they did not participate in active service.

Conclusions.
Scarcity of volunteers and the great number of negro slaves who had attached themselves to the Union Army, coupled with the fact that as freeman there was a demand both sentimental and practical that they should participate in the burdens of war, caused the raising of negro troops. It was a natural sequence to the Emancipation Proclamation.

Such evidence as was examined showed that when well led by white officers their service was very creditable. Where they failed poor leadership was almost certainly to be found.

The Indian Wars.
With the reduction of the Regular Army after the Civil War and the reorganization of 1869 four regiments of colored troops were formed in the Regular Army, the 24th and 25th Infantry, the 9th and 10th Cavalry. Their officers have been white, except in a few scattered instances. These regiments participated in several of the Indian Campaigns and skirmishes. There service was credible.

Conclusions.
The negro organizations always consisted of small companies and troops commanded by experienced white officers and in the ranks were many noncommissioned officers and soldiers of long service. Habits of discipline and confidence in their officers was largely responsible for their good service.

Spanish American War.

On the outbreak of war there were four regular regiments in the service, the 24th and 25th Infantry, the 9th and 10th Cavalry. These had white officers throughout, while in the ranks were noncommissioned officers, most of whom had several enlistments; and indeed many of the private soldiers also had long services. All four of these regiments participated in the Santiago Campaign, suffered losses and all did good service according to all reports.

In addition to the regular regiments five State volunteer regiments and four-so-called Immune Regiments were raised. None of these regiments had active service. Most of these volunteer regiments had white officers in the higher grades, but a few had colored officers throughout. As those did not get into action no opportunity was given to test their combat value.

Conclusions.

No separate organization larger than a regiment of colored troops participated in the war. Even these regiments were approximately the size of a battalion under our modern system of organization. The character of leadership of white officers, the length of service of the enlisted men, the discipline of the regular troops and the offensive character of the campaigns against a much inferior enemy did not put the negro troops to the severe test that modern war would demand of the hastily raised troops that compose a national army. While the service of the colored regular regiments was satisfactory, it is far from conclusive as to what might be expected of new troops under more trying conditions and less efficient leadership.

Philippine Insurrection.

All four of the regular regiments participated at some time in the campaign against the Philippine Insurgents. None of them were present during the earlier months when the organized armies of the Insurrectos were in the field. The personnel of these regiments were practically the same type as during the Spanish War.

In addition two volunteer regiments, the 48th and 49th were raised and saw service. In these the company officers were colored, being chosen largely from the noncommissioned officers of the regular regiments. All field and staff officers were white, the former being Regular Army officers.

While all colored troops saw service they did not suffer any serious losses. A number of officers have commented on the fact that where there was more or less continual sniping at sentries, particularly at night, the morale of the colored troops became appreciably lower than that in white organizations. There was also a tendency to affiliate with the natives, and there were some desertions to the insurgents.

Conclusions.

The character of service of the colored troops in the Philippines was not such that definite conclusions could be drawn as to their values as modern combat soldiers.

The World War.

During the World War 367,710 negroes were inducted into the service of the United States. They were organized into service and labor battalions, pioneer regiments of infantry; into one complete division the 92nd, and the so-called 93d Division, which in fact consisted of four separate infantry regiments. These two divisions were the only colored combat troops that actually saw front line service. The history of these two organizations is of particular importance as the facts are easily accessible and offer first-hand evidence of the action of negro troops in modern combat, when organized in large units.

Briefly, the history of the 92nd Division is as follows: Organization started October 26, 1917, in seven different cantonments. The General Field and Staff officers were white, chosen from the Regular Army; originally company officers of infantry, artillery, (except the heavy regiment) engineers and machine gun units were colored, most of them graduates from the colored training camp at Des Moines, Iowa. Prior to departure from the United States the inefficiency of the negro officers of artillery caused them to be replaced by whites; and this was also done in the Engineers on arrival in France. It may be stated here that the colored officers training camp was for Infantry, and that many of the candidates were ex-noncommissioned officers of the Regular Army. It is a fact attested by all that the educational qualifications of these negro officers were far below the standards required for white officers. The enlisted personnel was well above the average run of the draft due to selective methods. Particularly was this true in the heavy artillery regiment and the Signal Battalion where efforts were made to have specially qualified men inducted into the service.

The division was brought to full strength just before embarkation, and sailed for France in June, 1918, where it went into a training area and spent seven weeks, the training being assisted by the assignment of a number of French officers and noncommissioned officers. From there it went on the line in the quiet St. Dis Sector, remaining until September 20, when it was withdrawn by

rail and thus proceeded to the Argonne and became reserve for the 1st American Corps. One regiment, the 368th Infantry, was detached for duty as liaison group under the French 38th Corps and operated between that Corps and the left of the American forces. It was the only regiment that actually participated in the battle. A detailed study of its action has been made by the Historical Section of the Army War College. It is enough to say that it was on the line from September 25 to September 29, that it failed to make its objectives, withdrew without orders and became badly demoralized. The regimental commander showed that the principal cause of the failure was the inefficiency of the colored officers, and requested that 35 of them be removed for inefficiency and cowardice. Five of them were later convicted by General Court Martial for cowardice. The entire division was withdrawn and sent to the Marbache Area, another quiet sector. Here it remained until after the Armistice, taking part in the attacks of the 2nd Army on November 10 and 11, operations of a minor character, but in which the division made an advance of about 2 kilometers, but nowhere was serious resistance encountered. The division showed a marked improvement over its work in the Argonne. The artillery which joined the division in the Marbache Sector gave fairly efficient support.

Of the various units in the division, the artillery and engineers had a fair degree of efficiency. The trains were well handled and transportation kept in better condition than in most white organizations. The Signal Battalion was never equal to its task due to inability to obtain electricians, radio and telegraph operators. The infantry was never to be considered first-class. The Commander of the French Division under whom the 368th operated reported it as useless for combat.

A great deal of dissatisfaction among the negro soldiers and officers was fomented by negro agitators and magazines which continually attempted to force the race issue and bring forward claims for social equality.

To summarize, the 92nd Division failed as a first-class combat unit, but nevertheless performed useful service on the defensive in quiet sectors.

The 93rd Division consisted of the 369th, 370th, 371st and 372nd Infantry Regiments. They were detached for duty with the French Army and always operated as parts of a French Division. The 369th was originally the 15th New York and had a number of colored officers, all of whom were ultimately removed, some of them being sent to the 92nd Division. The 370th a former Illinois National Guard regiment, during active service was commanded by a regular officer of long service with colored troops. In the 371st all officers were white. In the 372nd originally there were many colored officers but most of these were ultimately eliminated. These four regiments saw service and did creditable work as combat troops, but according to reports were not as efficient as our white troops nor the French.

Conclusions.

1. The large number of negroes inducted into the service as a result of the draft necessitated their being organized into various types of units. The demand for service and labor troops was met by assignment of many of the uneducated ignorant negroes. The 92nd Division was organized as a result of political pressure upon the administration. Political considerations also caused the formation of the negro training camp and the commissioning of some six hundred as officers.

2. As combat troops under modern war conditions they never rose to the standard of white units even when well led by white officers. The negro officers were educationally and in character far inferior to the whites, and troops under negro officers were unfit for battle against an aggressive active enemy.

3. As non-combatants in service and labor units and as drivers of animal and motor transport they did good service.

4. When grouped into units larger than a regiment they did not succeed, as thereby they lost touch with and sight of the white troops as examples and supports.

5. No attempt was made to group negroes and whites in the same units, except that in some service units white noncommissioned officers were used as overseers, and successfully.

Commanding Officer, 371st Infantry, "In a future war the main use of the negro should be in labor organizations. Before leaving for France a request for 25% extra officers was granted and permitted the greatest use of white leadership."

Commanding Officer 372nd Infantry, "My observation of the Negro soldier leads me to believe that his services would be best utilized with labor troops or pioneer engineers. If circumstances require them to be organized into combat organizations, then combatant officers should all be white – also the non-commissioned officers."

Commanding Officer, 317th Engineers, "After the negro lieutenants of the regiment were replaced by white the improvement was such that its efficiency was but little less than that of the average white engineer regiment."

Commanding Officer, 167th Field Artillery Brigade, "As motor mechanics, both in their handling of the tractors and trucks, the negroes were, in my opinion, fully as good if not better than white troops. In regard to personal equation it was my feeling that the men, if properly lead were equal to any task to which they were set."

Commanding Officer, 350th Field Artillery, "The men compared better than favorably with the white brigade as regards to exposure to influenza and pneumonia. The conduct of the regiment under shell fire was satisfactory. The presence of a large body of discontented negros in the U.S. trained in the use of arms offers an inviting field for enemy propaganda."

Commanding Officer, 351st Field Artillery, "I believe the artillery of the 92nd Division made good in every way while at the front. In general colored troops should be used as labor units with the ultimate goal of front line troops for the most trustworthy and intelligent."

6. One of the most striking and significant features of the employment of negro soldiers, in all of the countries considered, is the uniform and emphatic conviction that negro troops are efficient and dependable only so long as led by capable white officers and noncommissioned officers. The reasons for this are not generally discussed in the reference consulted but may be ascribed to the following:

(a) Low intellectual capacity.
(b) Insufficient technical education.
(c) Lack of leading men of officer material.

(d) Lack of confidence of colored troops in officers of their own race.
(e) The questionable wisdom of training military leaders for armed peoples of a race, in their present development, who are not considered capable of exercising beneficial control in their various communities.

IV. <u>Conclusions.</u>

In addition to certain special conclusions appearing in the discussion, the following general conclusions are drawn from the study:

1. That negro troops, in countries other than the United States, are employed largely for the protection and police of colonial possessions. In France they are employed to augment the insufficient manpower and ease the financial burden of national defense.

2. That negro troops in the United States are employed in war both from political reasons and from the standpoint that the negro citizen should share the responsibilities, burdens and dangers of the war-time activities of his country.

3. That under efficient white leadership negro troops have done effective combat service.

4. Under negro officers they have displayed entire ineptitude for modern battle. Their natural racial characteristics, lack of initiative and tendency to become panic stricken, can only be overcome when they have confidence in their leaders.

5. They are much more susceptible to panic and their morale is quickly lowered when they come under shell fire or suffer physical hardships.

6. Their principal use during the World War was that for which they are best fitted, via., as service and labor troops, but with selected men under competent leadership they will become useful combat troops but not equal to American white soldiers.

ENDNOTES

Introduction

[1] William Allison Sweeny, *History of the American Negro in the Great World War*, G.G. Sapp: Chicago, 1919, p. 85.

[2] Ibid. p. 86

[3] Ibid. p. 91

[4] Ibid. p. 94

[5] William Gladstone, *Men of Color*, Thomas Publications: Gettysburg, Pennsylvania, p. 3.

[6] William Allison Sweeny, *History of the American Negro in the Great World War*, G.G. Sapp: Chicago, 1919, p. 97.

[7] Ibid, p. 98.

[8] Emmitt J. Scott, *The American Negro in the World War*, E.J.Scott: Washington ,D.C.,1919. p. 24.

[9] U.S. Army Heritage and Education Center, Military History Institute World War I Veteran Survey Collection. Supply Sergeant Austin M. Roberts, 365th Infantry Regiment, 92nd Division.

[10] Emmitt J. Scott, *The American Negro in the World War*, E.J.Scott: Washington ,D.C.,1919. p. 344.

[11] Ibid, p. 64.

Chapter 1 Notes

[1] OB pp. 27-80.

[2] Emmitt J. Scott, *The American Negro in the World War*, Privately published, 1919, p 316.

[3] OB, p. 31.

[4] Department of War, Tables of Organization and Equipment U.S. Army, Volume 3, 1918, Table 302.

[5] Addie W. Hunton and Kathryn M. Johnson, *Two Colored Women with the American Expeditionary Forces*, G.K. Hall & Company, New York, N.Y., 1997, p136.

[6] OB pp 1349-1354 and *Historical Report of the Chief Engineer including all operations of the Engineer Department American Expeditionary Forces 1917-1919*, Washington, D.C.: Government Printing Office, 1919.

[7] Tom Fife Collection, research papers.

[8] OB, pp. 1402-1403, Moses N. Thisted, Pershing's Pioneer Infantry of World War I, Hemet, California: Alphabet Printers, 1982, pp. 182-183.

[9] Department of War, Tables of Organization and Equipment U.S. Army, Volume 1, 1918, Table 103.

[10] Addie W. Hunton and Kathryn M. Johnson, *Two Colored Women with the American Expeditionary Forces*, G.K. Hall & Company, New York, N.Y., 1997, p157.

[11] OB pp 1402-1403.

[12] OB, p 1480.

[13] Department of War, Tables of Organization and Equipment U.S. Army, Volume 3, 1918, Table 358.

[14] Edward S. Farrow, *A Dictionary of Military Terms*, New York: Thomas Y. Crowell Company, 1918. p.586.

[15] Department of War, Tables of Organization and Equipment U.S. Army, Volume 3, 1918, Table 403.

[16] OB, pp. 1517-1518.

[17] Department of War, Tables of Organization and Equipment U.S. Army, Volume 3, 1918, Table 346.

[18] Department of War, Tables of Organization and Equipment U.S. Army, Volume 3, 1918, Table 329.

[19] OB, pp 1501 -1506.

[20] Department of War, Tables of Organization and Equipment U.S. Army, Volume 3, 1918, Table 316.

[21] Farrow, p. 333.

[22] OB, 1523.

[23] Department of War, Tables of Organization and Equipment U.S. Army, Volume 3, 1918, Table 328.

[24] Department of War, Tables of Organization and Equipment U.S. Army, Volume 3, 1918, Table 403.

[25] John B. Wilson, *Armies, Corps, Divisions, and Separate Brigades*, Center or Military History: Washington, DC, 1993, p. 10.

[26] Steve and Dave Johnson, *The Evolution of Shoulder Patches in the U.S. Army from 1918 to 2000*, a paper presented to members of the Association of American Insignia Collectors, 2000.

[27] Wilson, p. 13.

[28] Ibid, p. 13.

[29] Wilson, pp. 15-16.

[30] OB, p. 1351-1354.

[31] Historical Report of the Chief Engineer including all Operations of the Engineer Department American Expeditionary Forces 1917-1919, Washington, D.C.: Government Printing Office, 1919, p. 118.

[32] OB, pp. 1402-1403.

[33] Historical Report of the Chief Engineer including all Operations of the Engineer Department American Expeditionary Forces 1917-1919, Washington, D.C.: Government Printing Office, 1919, p. 118.

[34] Major Paul S. Bliss, *History of the 805th Pioneer Infantry American Expeditionary Forces*, St. Paul, Minnesota: Privately Published, 1920.

[35] Addie W. Hunton and Kathryn M. Johnson, *Two Colored Women with the American Expeditionary Forces*, G.K. Hall & Company, New York, N.Y., 1997, pp.142-146.

[36] Ibid, p. 166.

[37] Ibid, pp.152-153.

[38] Ibid, p 157.

[39] Ibid, p. 154.
[40] Ibid, p 158.
[41] Wilson, 47.
[42] Ibid, 48.
[43] Wilson, p. 51.
[44] Ibid, p. 52.
[45] Wilson, p. 55.
[46] Ibid, 56.
[47] Wilson, p. 59.
[48] Ibid, p. 60.
[49] Wilson, p. 64.
[50] Ibid, p. 64.
[51] Wilson, p. 67.
[52] Ibid, p. 68.
[53] Wilson, p. 72.
[54] Ibid, p. 72.
[55] Wilson, p. 75.
[56] Wilson, p. 78.

Chapter 2 Notes

[1] Castlebled, p. 154.
[2] CP, pp. 54-55.
[3] African-Americans in the Great War, Military Images, Volume XXVII, Number 4, p. 9.
[4] BPOAEF, pp. 81-95.
[5] OB, p. 429.
[6] BHD, pp. 83-84.
[7] AABE, pp. 515-517.
[8] Scott, Emmett J. *The American Negro in the World War*, p. 173. 1919, Emmet J. Scott
[9] Ibid, p. 173
[10] Ibid, pp193-194
[11] Ibid, pp165-166.
[12] Ibid, p. 166.
[13] Ibid, p. 167.
[14] Ibid, p. 168.
[15] Torrence, Gerald, *No Excuses: African-American Service in World War I*, Arm Chair General, TBP.
[16] Ibid.
[17] Castlebled, p. 156.
[18] Military Images, p. 18.
[19] CP, pp. 56-57.
[20] BPOAEF, pp. 81-104.
[21] OB, p. 359.
[22] BHD, pp. 95-97.
[23] Department of War, Tables of Organization and Equipment U.S. Army, Volume 3, Table 308.

Chapter 3 Notes

[1] Spingarn was a liberal Republican who helped settle a dispute between W.E.B. DuBois, whom he'd known at Harvard, and the followers of Booker T. Washington. He helped realize the concept of a unified black movement through the founding of the NAACP, the National Association for the Advancement of Colored People and was one of the first Jewish leaders of the NAACP, its second president, and chairman of its board from 1913 until his death.
[2] Charles Johnson, Jr. African Americans and ROTC, Jefferson, North Carolina: McFarland & Company, Inc., 2002. pp. 11-12.

Chapter 4 Notes

[1] For details of the reorganization of the Army which included the new black regiments see, John B. Wilson, Maneuver and Firepower The Evolution of Divisions and Separate Brigades, Washington, D.C., Center of Military History, 1998.
[2] There is a detailed treatment of the Regular Army black units in the following texts; Barbeau, Arthur E. & Henri, Florette. *TheUnknown Soldiers*. Temple University Press, Philadelphia, 1974, Henri, Florette. *Bitter Victory, A History of Black Soldiers in World War I*. Zenith Books, Doubleday & Company, Inc. Garden City, N.J. 1970, Scott, Emmett. *Scott's Official History of the American Negro in the World War*. Emmett J. Scott, 1919.Sweeny, W. Allison. *History of the American Negro in the Great World War*. G.G. Sapp, 1919.
[3] OB, pp1351-1355.
[4] Department of War, Tables of Organization and Equipment U.S. Army, Volume 3, 1918, Table 302.
[5] OB, pp. 1402-1403, Moses N. Thisted, Pershing's Pioneer Infantry of World War I, Hemet, California: Alphabet Printers, 1982, pp. 182-183.
[6] Department of War, Tables of Organization and Equipment U.S. Army, Volume 1, 1918, Table 103.
[7] OB, 1505-1510.
[8] Department of War, Tables of Organization and Equipment U.S. Army, Volume 3, 1918, Table 316.
[9] Edward S. Farrow, A Dictionary of Military Terms, New York: Thomas Y. Crowell Company, 1918. P 333.
[10] OB, p. 1355.
[11] Department of War, Tables of Organization and Equipment U.S. Army, Volume 3, 1918, Table 310.
[12] OB, p. 1278-1307.
[13] George Edmund Haynes, *The Trend of the Races*. New York: Council of Women for Home Missions and Missionary Education movement of the United States and Canada, 1923. p 123.
[14] National Archives II, College Park, Maryland, Record Group 407,War Department Files World War I Organization Files, Number 130.
[15] Military History Institute, Carlisle, PA, War Department, Historical Section Correspondence File Number 2957.
[16] Military History Institute, Carlisle, PA, War Department, Historical Section Correspondence File Number 2957.
[17] Military History Institute, Carlisle, PA, War Department, Historical Section Correspondence File Number 2957.

BIBLIOGRAPHY

Primary Sources: First person Accounts, Manuscripts, Letters, Diaries, Speeches, Interviews and Other Material.

Brief Histories of Divisions, U.S. Army 1917-1918. A study prepared by the Historical Branch of the War Plans Division of the Army General Staff, 1921.

Tom Fife Collection, Spotsylvania, Virginia.

National Archives, College Park, Maryland, Record Group 407,War Department Files World War I Organization Files, Number 130.

World War I Veterans Survey Collection, Army Heritage Museum and US Army Military History Institute, US Army Heritage and Education Center, Carlisle, Pennsylvania.

War Department, American Expeditionary Forces, After Action Reports, 1919.

War Department, Tables of Organization and Equipment, U.S. Army, 1918.

Published Sources (Books)

American Battle Monuments Commission, *American Armies and Battlefields in Europe,* Washington, DC: U.S. Government Printing Office, 1938.

Barbeau, Arthur E. & Henri, Florette. *The Unknown Soldiers.* Philadelphia: Temple University Press, 1974.

Bliss, Paul S., *History of the 805th Pioneer Infantry American Expeditionary Forces*, St. Paul, Minnesota: Privately Published, 1920.

Complete United States Infantry Guide. Philadelphia, Pennsylvania: J.B. Lippincott Company, 1917.

Castelbled, Maurice de. *History of the A.E.F.* New York: Bookcraft, 1937.

Emerson, William K. *Encyclopedia of United States Army Insignia and Uniforms*, Norman and London: University of Oklahoma Press, 1996.

Farrow, Edward S. *A Dictionary of Military Terms.* New York: Thomas Y. Crowell Company, 1918.

Gladstone, William, *Men of Color*, Thomas Publications: Gettysburg, Pennsylvania, 1996.

Haynes, George Edmund, *The Trend of the Races.* New York: Council of Women for Home Missions and Missionary Education movement of the United States and Canada, 1923.

Henri, Florette. *Bitter Victory, A History of Black Soldiers in World War I.* Zenith Books, Doubleday & Company, Inc. Garden City, N.J. 1970.

Huton, Addie & Johnson, Kathryn M., *Two Colored Women with the American Expeditionary Forces,* New York: G.K. Hall & Company, 1997.

Historical Section U.S. Army War College, *Order of Battle of the United States Land Forces in the World War: American Expeditionary Forces: Divisions*, Washington, DC: United States Government Printing Office, 1931.

Johnson, Charles Jr. *African Americans and ROTC*, Jefferson, North Carolina: McFarland & Company, Inc, 2002.

Keller, William & Keller, Kurt. United States Shoulder Patches and Related Insignia World War I to Korea, 1st Division to 40th Division, Atglen, Pennsylvania: Schiffer Publishing, 2002.

Keller, William & Keller, Kurt. *United States Shoulder Patches and Related Insignia World War I to Korea, Army Groups, Armies and Corps*, Atglen, Pennsylvania: Schiffer Publishing, 2004.

Keller, William & Keller, Kurt. *United States Shoulder Patches and Related Insignia World War I to Korea, 41st to 106th Division*, Atglen, Pennsylvania: Schiffer Publishing, 2002.

The Medical Department of the United States in the World War, 16 Volumes. Washington, DC: Government Printing Office, 1923.

Sweeny, William Allison, *The History of the American Negro in the Great World War*, Chicago: G.G. Sapp, 1919.

Thisted, Moses N., *Pershing's Pioneer Infantry of World War One*, Hemet, California: Alphabet Printers, 1982.

United States Army in the World War 1917-1919, 17 Volumes. Washington, DC: Center of Military History, 1988.

United States Army in the World War, 1917-1919, Organization of the American Expeditionary Forces, 3 Volumes, Washington, DC: Center of Military History, 1988.

War Office United States of America, *Battle Participation of Organizations of the American Expeditionary Forces in France, Belgium and Italy 1917-1918.* Washington, DC: United States Government Printing Office, 1920.

Wilson, John B. *Armies, Corps, Divisions, and Separate Brigades*, Washington, DC: Center or Military History, 1993.

Wilson, John B. *Maneuver and Firepower The Evolution of Divisions and Separate Brigades*, Washington, DC: Center or Military History, 1998.

Magazines, Periodicals, Pamphlets, and Miscellany

American Decorations and Insignia of Honor and Service, National Geographic, Volume XXXVI, Number Six.

American Society of Military Insignia Collectors, *Cloth Patch of the U.S. Armed Forces: Divisions.* American Society of Military Insignia Collectors: 1968.

African-Americans in the Great War, Military Images, Volume XXVII, Number 4.